MINISTERIAL ORDERS AND SACRAMENTAL AUTHORITY
IN THE UNITED METHODIST CHURCH AND ITS ANTECEDENTS
1784–2016

REX D. MATTHEWS

Ministerial Orders and Sacramental Authority in The United Methodist Church and Its Antecedents, 1784–2016

The General Board of Higher Education and Ministry leads and serves The United Methodist Church in the recruitment, preparation, nurture, education, and support of Christian leaders—lay and clergy—for the work of making disciples of Jesus Christ for the transformation of the world. Its vision is that a new generation of Christian leaders will commit boldly to Jesus Christ and be characterized by intellectual excellence, moral integrity, spiritual courage, and holiness of heart and life. The General Board of Higher Education and Ministry of The United Methodist Church serves as an advocate for the intellectual life of the church. The Board's mission embodies the Wesleyan tradition of commitment to the education of laypersons and ordained persons by providing access to higher education for all persons.

Wesley's Foundery Books is named for the abandoned foundery that early followers of John Wesley transformed, which later became the cradle of London's Methodist movement.

HIGHER EDUCATION & MINISTRY
General Board of Higher Education and Ministry
THE UNITED METHODIST CHURCH

Contents

Introduction

This study traces the changing provisions relating to ministerial orders and sacramental authority in American Methodism, from the formation of the Methodist Episcopal Church (MEC) in 1784 to the current position of The United Methodist Church (UMC) as contained in *The United Methodist Book of Discipline* 2016. Particular attention is given to the debates about sacramental authority in the 1922 and 1926 General Conferences of the Methodist Episcopal Church, South (MECS) and at the 1939 Uniting Conference, which brought back together the Methodist Episcopal Church (MEC), the MECS, and the Methodist Protestant Church (MPC) to form The Methodist Church (MC). Coming into that merger, both the MECS and the MPC allowed unordained preachers appointed as pastors of a church or charge to administer the sacraments of baptism and the Lord's Supper within the bounds of their charge and to perform marriages where state law allowed. In contrast, the MEC allowed unordained preachers to baptize and marry (subject to state law) but not to administer the Lord's Supper. The debate about ministerial orders and sacramental authority at the 1939 General Conference set the stage for later discussion about and action on these issues in The Methodist Church and, after 1968, in The United Methodist Church.

Karen B. Westerfield Tucker outlines some of the story told here in the chapter "Roles in Public Worship" in her history of *American Methodist Worship*, as does Dennis M. Campbell in his essay on "Ministry and Itinerancy in Methodism" in *The Oxford Handbook of Methodist Studies,* and E. Brooks Holifield in his essay on "Clergy" in *The Cambridge Companion to American Methodism.*[1] In all three cases, however, limitations of space necessarily place constraints on their accounts. Recent full-length discussions of United Methodist polity in general—by Thomas E. Frank and Laceye C. Warner—and of the ordained ministry in particular—by Dennis M. Campbell, John E. Harnish, and William B. Lawrence—all give some attention to the historical development of ministerial orders and sacramental authority in The United Methodist Church and its antecedents.[2] The

---

1 Karen B. Westerfield Tucker, *American Methodist Worship* (New York: Oxford University Press, 2001), 257–69; Dennis M. Campbell, "Ministry and Itinerancy in Methodism," in *The Oxford Handbook of Methodist Studies*, ed. William J. Abraham and James E. Kirby (New York: Oxford University Press, 2009), 262–69; E. Brooks Holifield, "Clergy," in *The Cambridge Companion to American Methodism*, ed. Jason E. Vickers (New York: Cambridge University Press, 2013), 171–87. See also Holifield, *God's Ambassadors: A History of the Christian Clergy in America* (Grand Rapids: Wm. B. Eerdmans, 2007).

2 Thomas Edward Frank, *Polity, Practice, and the Mission of The United Methodist Church*, 2006 ed. (Nashville: Abingdon Press, 2006); Laceye W. Warner, *The Method of Our Mission: United Methodist Polity and Organization* (Nashville: Abingdon Press, 2014); Dennis M. Campbell, *Who Will Go for Us? An Invitation to Ordained Ministry* (Nashville: Abingdon Press, 1994); John E. Harnish, *The Orders of Ministry in The United Methodist Church* (Nashville: Abingdon Press, 2000); William B. Lawrence, *Ordained Ministry in The United Methodist Church* (Nashville: Abingdon Press, 2011).

primary focus of these works is on the contemporary realities of United Methodism, and thus they are not able to provide the depth of analysis and level of detailed discussion that this study seeks to provide.

This study features an unusually large number of lengthy quotations, many of them drawn from the accounts of discussions and debates preserved (often in surprising detail) in the *Daily Christian Advocate* and the *Journals* of the General Conferences during which they occurred. It seems important to enable readers of the study to enter as fully as possible into the conversation about the issues addressed here in the words of the participants themselves; hence the florilegium of quotations.

Thanks are due to the staff of three remarkable libraries for assistance with the research on which the study is based: the Pitts Theology Library at Candler School of Theology, Emory University; the Divinity Library at Duke Divinity School; and the United Methodist Archives and History Center of the General Commission on Archives and History of The UMC on the campus of Drew University. Thanks are also due to Candler School of Theology for grants of research leave in fall 2014 and spring 2017; to Duke Divinity School for an invitation to participate in the 2014 Summer Wesley Seminar; and to Drew University for a Florence Bell Scholar Award, which made possible two weeks of residential research in fall 2014 at the United Methodist Archives and History Center in Madison, New Jersey. Richard P. Heitzenrater, Russell E. Richey, Randy L. Maddox, and Ted A. Campbell all made helpful editorial suggestions along the way, and I thank them for their comments, which considerably strengthened the study. Kyle Tau proved to be a very sharp-eyed proofreader, and I am grateful to him for noting numerous typographical errors and stylistic infelicities in the penultimate draft. And last but certainly not least, thanks are due to my research assistants, Chris Black

(2014–2015) and Linda Stephan (2016–2017), for their valuable work on this and a related project.

The usual abbreviations are used here for the major American Methodist denominational bodies: MEC for the Methodist Episcopal Church, MPC for the Methodist Protestant Church, UMC for The United Methodist Church, and so on. In addition, JCG is used for *Journal of the General Conference*, DCA is used for *Daily Christian Advocate*, and *Discipline* is used for *The Book of Discipline* (in earlier eras, *Doctrines and Discipline*). These abbreviations are combined with the denominational abbreviations and years as in the following examples:

MECS/JGC 1906: Methodist Episcopal Church, South, *Journal of the General Conference*, 1906.

MC/DCA 1939: The Methodist Church, *Daily Christian Advocate*, General Conference, 1939.

UMC *Discipline* 2012: *The Book of Discipline of The United Methodist Church*, 2012.

Finally, a note about the title of this work. Taylor Burton-Edwards, the former director of worship resources for the General Board of Discipleship and a member of the Commission for the Study of Ministry for the 2012–2016 quadrennium, has argued that the language of *sacramental authority* should be stricken from the United Methodist theological lexicon, even when used as a kind of shorthand:

In the circles in The United Methodist Church where I have been blessed to travel, when I hear us talking about "sacramental authority," it almost always partakes of a rhetoric of rights and privileges unique to elders. Elders have sacramental authority, but deacons (with some case by case exceptions) do not. Local pastors have sacramental authority, but only within the bounds of the congregations or extension ministries to which they are appointed. The elder alone has "full" sacramental authority. Deacons may have "it" (that special, magical "it") contingently, if at all. And the laity have it not at all.

The language of sacramental authority "nouns" or "substantializes" as a "thing" [that] elders "have" what the Ordinal itself frames as an infinitive verb depicting a key part of the work we need elders to undertake as part of their way of life among us: "to administer the Holy Sacraments." In this "substantialization" or "reification," "sacramental authority" has come thus not to signify the fulfillment of the role of administering the sacraments named in our Ordinal, but rather its radical truncation. Why? Because when we are speaking of "sacramental authority" what we are too often really talking about is the "right" or "special power" of certain "magic people" to say certain "magic words" over ordinary things to make them into magical things. The language of "sacramental authority" and the consequent specifications of who has "it" and who does not, and under what conditions even those who have "it" may exercise "it," moves us and all of our thinking into the stasis of fixed rules rather than the "nephesh hayah" dynamics (and blessed messiness!) of living, Spirit-breathing community. And so we move straight into the cul-de-sac Greek substantialist ontologies rather than remaining in the flow of our ever-living, ever-moving, ever-dynamic biblical ontology.[3]

---

3   Taylor Burton-Edwards, "Ordination, Pneumatology and Ontology, Part 3: Ordination and Sacramental Authority"; https://blog.umc discipleship.org/ordination-pneumatology-and-ontology-part-3 -ordination-and-sacramental-authority/, accessed December 18, 2017.

While granting the force of Burton-Edwards's argument about ways in which the language of *sacramental authority* can be, and perhaps has been, misunderstood and misused, I cannot agree with his proposal that the language of *sacramental authority* should be entirely abandoned by contemporary United Methodists. As I think the present work will show in some depth and detail, that language is deeply interwoven in our richly textured history; it has been a significant element of the history of Christian ecumenical conversations about ordained ministry and sacramental administration. My hope for this small volume is that it will enable readers to trace at least the main contours of the long series of debates within American Methodism about issues related to orders of ministry and administration of the sacraments, thereby providing a richer appreciation and deeper understanding of the context of contemporary discussion of these issues. The historical, theological, sacramental, and spiritual threads of this tapestry became rather badly tangled at a number of points, and our Methodist forebears struggled with these interrelated issues in ways that are remarkably similar to our own efforts to come to grips with them. If this little book sheds even a small amount of light on the struggle to deal with these issues within United Methodism today, the labor that has gone into its creation will have been worthwhile.

The Methodist Episcopal Church (1784–1939)

The worldwide Methodist movement originated with the evangelistic work of brothers John and Charles Wesley beginning in England in 1739. The response of people to their preaching led to the formation of religious societies, first in Bristol and London, then elsewhere as the movement spread through industrializing English society and soon into Ireland. At first, these religious societies were modeled after those of the Moravians, but they soon developed their own distinctive patterns and practices. The Wesley brothers saw emergent Methodism as a reforming movement within the Church of England; they intended for it to serve as a supplement to, not a replacement for, the Church of England.

Methodism spread to the New World as English and Irish immigrants to America brought their Methodist beliefs and practices with them. By the late 1760s, Methodist societies existed in New York, Philadelphia, Baltimore, and surrounding regions. At the request of the American Methodists, John Wesley began sending preachers from England to America in 1769, and by 1773, Methodist work there was more formally organized. As the tensions between England and the American colonies increased, leading to revolution, the Church of England basically ceased to exist in America, creating a sacramental crisis: there were no ordained ministers to provide the sacraments to American Methodists.

Failing to find another resolution to this crisis, in 1784, John Wesley took the irregular action of ordaining two of his lay preachers for service in America, and of "setting apart" Thomas Coke (who was already an ordained presbyter of the Church of England) to be "general superintendent" of American Methodism along with Francis Asbury (who had been in America since 1771). This led to the establishment of the Methodist Episcopal Church (MEC) in America, with Coke and Asbury as the first bishops.[1]

As a consequence of its origins, American Methodism has always had what Tom Frank aptly describes as a "dual framework" for ministry. Prior to the establishment of the MEC as an autonomous church in 1784, the preaching ministry was primary; one became a Methodist preacher by trial and approval and acceptance as a member of the conference. None of the Methodist preachers in America were ordained, and the Methodist people were expected (at least in theory) to have access to the sacraments through the ordained ministry of the Church of England. Things changed after 1784, and the status conferred by ordination gradually became the distinguishing mark of a Methodist minister:

> After 1784 the Methodist Episcopal Church made a subtle distinction between "ministers" and "preachers."

---

1   See Richard P. Heitzenrater, *Wesley and the People Called Methodists*, 2nd ed. (Nashville: Abingdon Press, 2013), 317–25; and Russell E. Richey, Kenneth E. Rowe, and Jean Miller Schmidt, *The Methodist Experience in America*, vol. 1: *A History* (Nashville: Abingdon Press, 2010), 33–72.

While both were first and foremost called to preach, the former were ordained full members of annual conference; the latter served in local churches and were neither ordained nor members of conference.[2]

At its formation in 1784, the MEC adopted a threefold structure of ordained ministry, consisting of bishops, elders, and deacons. However, unlike the Church of England, the MEC did not understand the episcopacy to be a distinct, separate, third ministerial order.[3] This was largely because the understanding that elders and bishops were of the same *order* and so had the same power of ordination was the basis of John Wesley's decision to ordain some of his preachers for service in North America in the wake of the American Revolution. Wesley, of course, was an elder (or presbyter) of the Church of England, not a bishop, but he claimed to have the same *right* to ordain as any bishop.[4] To complicate things further, Francis Asbury refused to accept appointment as "general superintendent,"

2   Frank, *Polity, Practice and the Mission of The United Methodist Church*, 197; cf. 195–99.

3   For an interesting discussion of this matter, see Byron Stuhlman, *Occasions of Grace: An Historical and Theological Study of the Pastoral Offices and Episcopal Services in the BCP* (New York: Church Publishing, 1995), 261–63.

4   See Linda M. Durbin, "The Nature of Ordination in Wesley's View of the Ministry," *Methodist History* 9 (April 1971): 3–20. Some of Wesley's concerns about ordination, and the responses of some of his preachers in the early 1760s, are helpfully discussed in Ted A. Campbell, "The Transgressions of Gerasimos Avlonites," Perkins Faculty Research and Special Events, Paper 3 (2015); http://digitalrepository.smu.edu/theology_research/3. There is, of course, a sizeable body of literature about Wesley's decision to ordain and its consequences, which will not be explored further here.

even at Wesley's explicit instruction, without being elected to that office by the other American preachers.

From the beginning, then, American Methodism has understood bishops to be elders who were elected to that office and then "set apart" or consecrated for service as "general superintendents." Bishops had distinctive administrative and supervisory responsibilities, including the appointment of preachers to circuits or stations and the ordination of others as elders or deacons, but their sacramental authority was the same as that of other members of the order of elders because in terms of their ordination that is what they were. Until 1996, deacons were understood to be a lower clerical order, with different rights and responsibilities; service for a probationary period as a deacon was understood to be a necessary transitional stage in the process leading to ordination as an elder.

The first *Discipline* of the MEC contained this language describing the offices of elder and deacon:

Q. 30. What is the office of an elder?

A. To administer the sacraments of baptism and the Lord's Supper, and to perform all the other rites prescribed by our Liturgy.

Q. 31. What is the office of a deacon?

A. To baptize in the absence of an elder, to assist the elder in the administration of the Lord's Supper, to marry, bury the dead, and read the Liturgy to the people as prescribed, except what relates to the administration of the Lord's Supper.[5]

The list of duties of both elders and deacons was soon elaborated, but this language about their sacramental authority

---

5   MEC *Discipline* 1785, 12.

was basically unchanged (save for the curious disappearance of "bury the dead" after 1787) until 1792, when the offices of "presiding elder" and "traveling elder" were first differentiated. Prior to 1792, all elders were understood to be "presiding" elders, in the sense of sacramental presidency. Those offices were now distinguished; a presiding elder was appointed by the bishop and had these principal responsibilities:

1. To travel through his appointed District.
2. In the absence of a Bishop, to take charge of all the Elders, Deacons, Traveling and Local Preachers, and Exhorters in his District.
3. To change, receive or suspend Preachers in his District during the intervals of the Conference, and in the absence of the Bishop.
4. In the absence of a Bishop, to preside in the Conference of his District.
5. To be present, as far as practicable, at all the Quarterly Meetings; and to call together at each Quarterly Meeting all the Traveling and Local Preachers, Exhorters, Stewards, and Leaders of the circuit, to hear complaints, and to receive appeals.[6]

The presiding elder was thus a sort of assistant bishop and the predecessor of the contemporary district superintendent. But, like bishops, presiding elders had exactly the same sacramental authority as that of other members of the order of elders, because in terms of their ordination that is what they were.

The duties of a traveling elder and a traveling deacon (both terms now used for the first time) are described as follows in the MEC *Discipline* 1792:

---

6   MEC *Discipline* 1792, 18.

Quest. What is the duty of a Traveling Elder?

Answ. 1. To administer Baptism and the Lord's Supper, to perform the office of matrimony, and all parts of divine worship. 2. To do all the duties of a Traveling Preacher.

Quest. What is the duty of a Traveling Deacon?

Answ. 1. To baptize, and to perform the office of matrimony, in the absence of the Elder. 2. To assist the Elder in administering the Lord's Supper. 3. To do all the duties of a Traveling Preacher.[7]

Also in 1792, a new section was introduced into the *Discipline* specifying "the Duties of those who have the charge of Circuits."[8] This list of duties grew longer through the years but dealt primarily with responsibilities related to administration and order.[9]

In their annotated edition of the MEC *Discipline* 1796, published in 1798, Bishops Coke and Asbury wrote at considerable length about the offices of bishop and presiding elder as understood in American Methodism. They found it unnecessary to say very much about the office of elder: "We need not enlarge upon the necessity of an office, which every organized Christian church in the World, in all ages, has adopted."[10] They

---

7   MEC *Discipline* 1792, 19–20.

8   MEC *Discipline* 1792, 24–26.

9   See Robert Emory, *History of the Discipline of The Methodist Episcopal Church*, fifth edition, revised and updated to 1856 by W. P. Stickland (New York: Carleton & Porter, 1857); and David Sherman, *History of the Revisions of the Discipline of the Methodist Episcopal Church* (New York: Nelson & Phillips, 1874).

10 Thomas Coke and Francis Asbury, *The Doctrines and Discipline of the Methodist Episcopal Church in America, with Explanatory Notes,*

had rather more to say about the office of deacon, including this description of its relationship to the office of elder in the Methodist system:

> This office [deacon] serves as an excellent probation for that of an elder. No preacher can be eligible to the office of an elder, till he has exercised the office of a deacon for two years, except in the case of missions. For we would wish to shew the utmost attention to the order of elders, and to have the fullest proof of the abilities, grace, and usefulness of those, who shall be, from time to time, proposed for so important an office as that of a presbyter in the church of God. And we judge, that the man who has proved himself a worthy member of our society, and a useful class-leader, exhorter, and local preacher, who has been approved of for two years as a traveling preacher on trial, and has faithfully served in the office of a traveling deacon for at least two years more—has offered such proof of fidelity and piety, as must satisfy every reasonable mind. But as this continent is exceedingly large, and will continually open to our conferences new missions for the spread of the gospel (perhaps for ages to come), we have, in the case of missions, given a discretionary power to the yearly conferences. We have thus been able, through the grace and providence of God, to constitute such a regular gradation in our ministry, as, we trust, will contribute highly to its purity, to the

---

10th ed. [hereafter MEC *Discipline* 1796] (Philadelphia: Henry Tuckness, 1798), 54.

dignity of the ministerial office, and to the advantage of our people.[11]

According to Robert Emory's *History of the Discipline of the Methodist Episcopal Church*, the first provision for the ordination of local preachers as deacons came in 1789, when the following statement was inserted into the section of the *Discipline* dealing with the duties of the bishop:

> The bishop has obtained liberty, by the suffrages of the conference, to ordain local preachers to the office of deacons, provided they obtain a testimonial from the society to which they belong, and from the stewards of the circuit, signed by three traveling preachers, three deacons, and three elders (one of them a presiding elder); the names of those being nominated being read in the conference previous to their ordination.[12]

In 1792 the clause about reading the names was eliminated, and the nature of the necessary testimonial was changed to require the signatures of "three elders, three deacons, and three traveling preachers." In 1796 a paragraph on the subject was added to the section of the *Discipline* on local preachers, saying that "A local preacher shall be eligible to the office of a deacon after he has preached for four years from the time he has obtained a regular license" and has obtained the required testimonial. The requirements of the testimonial continued to change until 1808, when it involved an examination of their characters and the approbation of the yearly conference, with a testimonial "from the quarterly meeting of their respective

---

11 MEC *Discipline* 1796, 56–57.
12 Emory, *History of the Discipline of the Methodist Episcopal Church*, 183.

circuits, after proper examination, signed by the president and countersigned by the secretary."[13]

In his *History of the Methodist Episcopal Church*, Nathan Bangs indicates that the office of local deacon was first created by the 1800 General Conference specifically to provide for the needs of African congregations:

> The bishops were authorized [in 1800] to ordain those African preachers, in the places where there were houses of worship for their use, who might be chosen by a majority of the male members of the society to which they belonged, and could procure a recommendation from the preacher in charge and his colleagues on the circuit, to the office of local deacons. The rule granting this authority was not incorporated among the printed regulations of the *Discipline*, but by a vote of the conference was only to stand on its records. Richard Allen, of Philadelphia, was the first colored man who received orders under this rule. Since that time, however, many in different places have been elected and consecrated, and since the General Conference of 1812, when the bishops were authorized to ordain local deacons to the office of elders, after four years' probation as deacons, several have been ordained elders.[14]

The problem with this account is that the version of the 1796 *Discipline* annotated by Bishops Coke and Asbury, published in 1798, contains a statement about limitations on the

---

13 Emory, *History of the Discipline of the Methodist Episcopal Church*, 184.

14 Nathan Bangs, *A History of the Methodist Episcopal Church*, vol. 2, *From the Year 1793 to the Year 1816* (New York: T. Mason & G. Lane, 1839), 97–98.

power of Methodist bishops to ordain that makes specific mention of a "local deacon":

> They not only have no power to ordain *a person for the episcopal office* till he be first elected by the general conference, but they possess no authority to ordain *an elder or a travelling deacon*, till he be first elected by a *yearly* conference; or a local deacon, till he obtain a testimonial, signifying the approbation of the society to which he belongs, countersigned by the general stewards of the circuit, three elders, three deacons, and three traveling preachers.[15]

In Section XXI, "Of the Local Preachers," the 1796 *Discipline* also makes specific provisions for the trial of "local preachers, local deacons, or local elders." The answer to this question begins with the statement, "If a charge be brought against a local preacher, or local deacon, or elder. . . ." Later in the same paragraphs, reference is made to the "local preacher, deacon, or elder."[16] This may be simply a case of lack of consistency or precision in the use of the term *local* in these sentences, but since Section XIX of the 1796 *Discipline*[17] makes similar provisions for the trial of traveling preachers, including elders and deacons, it seems fairly clear that a distinction is being made between *traveling* elders and deacons and *local* elders and deacons, implying that both of the latter two categories did, in fact, exist as early as 1796. Bishops Coke and Asbury do nothing to clarify this matter in their annotations.

According to Bangs, the 1812 General Conference then took the "next step," so to speak, after considerable debate,

---

15 MEC *Discipline* 1796, 44, italics original.
16 MEC *Discipline* 1796, 116–17, Quest. 3.
17 MEC *Discipline* 1796, 109–10.

and authorized the ordination of local deacons, after four years of service, as local elders, apparently with the understanding that they would clearly be distinguished from traveling elders:

> This measure elicited a very strong debate, in which the talent of the most able members was brought into requisition, both for and against it. Those who were in favor of the measure, contended that the services of such were needed in the various parts of the work, where the number of traveling elders were few, to administer the ordinances of baptism and the Lord's Supper, and to perform the ceremony of marriage and burial of the dead;—that being recognized by our church as ministers of the gospel, they were also entitled, equally with their traveling brethren, to full powers as elders in the Church of God;—and, as conferring them would add dignity and importance to their character, it would also increase their usefulness, and consequently attach them more strongly to their traveling brethren.
>
> To this it was answered that the ordination service implied a covenant transaction, in which the person receiving orders took upon himself the charge of the flock of Christ, which a local elder in our Church could not do, and therefore could not fulfil his covenant obligations, inasmuch as he did not, nor could he as a mere local minister, devote himself exclusively to the work of the ministry—that as to the right he had to full orders, we must distinguish between original, unalienable, and acquired rights, between civil, political, and ecclesiastical rights. As to original or natural right, no one pretended that a local or any other preacher had it;—as to acquired, according to the economy of our

Church he could not acquire it, because no such provision had been made as the reward of services, however meritorious, this being reserved for traveling preachers alone, who sacrificed their all of temporal emolument and devoted themselves entirely to the service of the Church;—as to civil or political right, he could claim none, as the civil polity of our country did not interfere in religious matters at all;—and therefore it only remained to inquire whether our local deacons had an ecclesiastical right to the order of elders; and this was the very question at issue, and therefore they could have none until it be given to them by the Church to which they belong. The question then must be decided, it was contended, on the principles of expediency and the probable utility of the measure; and the majority finally decided that the privilege ought to be granted them on this ground—*they might be needed*, and *might therefore be useful.*

Having thus decided in favor of granting them elders' orders, the following regulations were adopted as the conditions on which the bishops were permitted to confer them, which show plainly that this privilege was granted solely on the presumption that in every case where ordinations of this character were allowed, there was an imperious call for the services of such elders, and not because they could claim them as a *right* originating from their relation to the Church. The regulations were as follows:—

"A local deacon shall be eligible to the office of an elder, and on the following regulations and restrictions, *viz.*, he shall have preached four years from the time he was ordained a deacon; and shall obtain a

recommendation of two-thirds from the quarterly conference of which he is a member, signed by the president and counter-signed by the secretary, certifying his
qualifications in doctrine, discipline, talents, and useful-
ness; and the necessity of the official services of such
local elder in the circuit where he resides. He shall, if
he cannot be present, send to the annual conference a
note certifying his belief in the doctrine and discipline of
our Church: the whole being examined and approved
by the annual conference, he shall be ordained. Provided that no slaveholder shall be eligible to the office
of local elder, in any state or territory where the civil
laws will admit emancipation, and suffer the liberated
slave to enjoy his freedom."[18]

The "question and answer" format, inherited from the
"Large" *Minutes* of Wesley's time, continued to be used in MEC
Disciplines until 1872, when it was replaced by a direct statement format. The following language about the sacramental
authority of elders and deacons is from the 1872 *Discipline*;
aside from the format, it is basically unchanged from the language of the 1792 *Discipline*:

¶244. The duty of a Traveling Elder is,—1. To administer Baptism and the Lord's Supper, to solemnize Matrimony, and to conduct divine worship. 2. To do all the
duties of a Traveling Preacher.

---

18 Bangs, *A History of the Methodist Episcopal Church*, 2:314–16; cf.
Emory, *History of the Discipline*, 184, and MEC *Discipline* 1812,
75 (italics original). It is worth stressing the significance of Bangs's
statement that in the end the primary factors in the decision were
"the principles of *expediency* and the probable *utility* of the measure" (italics added).

¶249. The duty of a Traveling Deacon is,—1. To administer Baptism and solemnize Matrimony. 2. To assist the Elder in administering the Lord's Supper. 3. To do all the duties of a Traveling Preacher.[19]

There was no change in these provisions until 1892, when there was some significant textual revision, including the disappearance of the *traveling* and *local* designations for deacons and elders:

¶161. A Deacon has authority to preach; to conduct Divine Worship; to solemnize Matrimony; to administer Baptism; and to assist the Elder in administering the Lord's Supper.

¶164. An Elder has authority to preach; to conduct Divine Worship; to solemnize Matrimony; and to administer the sacraments of Baptism and the Lord's Supper.[20]

This appears to be the point at which the distinction between *traveling* and *local* elders and deacons began to disappear from MEC usage. The paragraph enumeration and pagination subsequently varied, but there was no significant change in the language about the sacramental authority of deacons and elders in the MEC *Discipline* from 1892 to 1936.

In 1912 the MEC General Conference received a report from the Committee on the State of the Church, recommending that unordained local pastors be authorized to administer the sacrament of baptism and solemnize the rite of matrimony in accordance with prevailing state law; this limited sacramental

---

19 MEC *Discipline* 1872, ¶244, p. 104; ¶249, p. 105.

20 MEC *Discipline* 1892, (deacons) ¶161, pp. 93–94; (elders) ¶164, p. 95.

authority was not to extend to the administration of the Lord's Supper:

> When an unordained preacher is received on trial in an Annual Conference, and is regularly appointed to a charge by a Bishop presiding in said Conference; or when a local preacher is not on trial, and is employed by the District Superintendent to supply a charge, in either case he shall be authorized, as long as the above condition remains, to administer the sacrament of baptism and to solemnize marriage according to the laws on the state in which he lives.[21]

This proposal came to the floor of the 1912 General Conference in the closing minutes of the final session. The account of the debate in the *Daily Christian Advocate* reports that there was "great confusion" at several points but provides little detail about the substance of the debate. After several attempts to amend or table the proposal failed, this amendment was proposed by George W. White:

> Mr. Chairman, I move to insert the word "alone" after the word "appointed," so that it shall read: "When an unordained preacher is received on trial in an Annual Conference, and is appointed alone." It often happens that an unordained man is appointed on a circuit to accompany a man who is ordained, and there is no necessity of giving him this power.[22]

After this amendment was approved, the whole report was approved by the General Conference,[23] and the sacramental

---

21 MEC/DCA 1912, 787.
22 MEC/DCA 1912, 787–88.
23 MEC/JGC 1912, 514–15, 639.

authorization was duly included in the MEC *Discipline* 1912 as ¶156. The authorization was also incorporated into ¶215.3:

> ¶215.3. An unordained Local Preacher, while serving as a regularly appointed Pastor of a Charge, shall be authorized to administer the rite of Baptism, and when the laws of the State permit, to solemnize matrimony.[24]

In the 1920 *Discipline*, this sacramental authorization was slightly revised to reflect the situation of foreign mission work (¶221.3, p. 169; cf. JGC/MEC 1920, p. 511), but was subsequently unchanged until 1939:

> ¶221.3 An unordained Local Preacher, only while serving as a regularly appointed Pastor of a Charge, shall be authorized to administer the rite of Baptism, and when the laws of the State permit, to solemnize matrimony, but in all foreign mission fields, power to authorize him to solemnize Matrimony shall rest in the Central Mission Conference in which he is a Pastor.[25]

Proposals were submitted to the MEC General Conference 1920 to "take the next step" and permit unordained local preachers serving under appointment as pastors to administer the Lord's Supper; these proposals were not approved (MEC/JGC 1920, pp. 404, 511). Similar proposals were made to MEC General Conferences in 1928, 1932, and 1936; in all cases the committee considering the proposals recommended non-concurrence, and the committee recommendations were approved without floor debate (MEC/JGC 1928, 413, 542; MEC/JGC 1932, 456, 583–84; MEC/JGC 1936, 327, 447).

---

24 MEC *Discipline* 1912, ¶215.3, p. 157; see also ¶156, p. 119.
25 MEC *Discipline* 1920, ¶221.3, p. 169.

The Methodist
Protestant Church
(1830–1939)

The Methodist Protestant Church (MPC) was formed in 1830 as a result of growing dissatisfaction with the episcopacy and the lack of lay representation in the conferences (both annual and general) of the MEC. Efforts had been made at the MEC General Conferences of 1816 and 1820 to make the position of presiding elder elective. These efforts failed, resulting in increasing tensions between the self-described "reformers" and their opponents, eventually leading to the withdrawal of the reformers from the MEC to form a new denominational body. From its foundation the MPC eliminated the offices of bishop and presiding elder from its polity, and provided for the admission of laymen to both annual and general conferences, but maintained the same doctrinal standards as the MEC and continued the ministerial orders of deacon and elder.

Since 1792 the MEC *Discipline* had contained a paragraph outlining "the Duties of those who have the charge of Circuits," who could be elders, deacons, or unordained preachers.[1] The MPC, having eliminated the office of bishop, used the title "superintendent" for this purpose:

---

1   MEC *Discipline* 1792, 24–26.

> The minister, who shall be appointed by the annual conference, to the charge of a station or circuit, shall be styled, the Superintendent; and shall be amenable to the annual conference for his official conduct.[2]

The first item in the list of duties of a superintendent involved sacramental authority:

> 1. It shall be the duty of the superintendent of a circuit or station, to fill the pulpits or have them filled, in accordance with the regulations of the quarterly conference; and to administer the ordinances, assisted by his brethren in the ministry.[3]

The MPC enshrined in its first *Discipline* the equality of all elders in the church as one of the eleven "elementary principles" that provided the foundation for its Constitution:

> The pastoral or ministerial office and duties are of divine appointment; and all elders in the church of God are equal; but ministers are forbidden to be lords over God's heritage, or to have dominion over the faith of the saints.[4]

Article X of the MPC Constitution also clearly and unambiguously stated that "No higher order of ministers shall be

---

2 MPC *Discipline* 1830, 27.

3 MPC *Discipline* 1830, 50. It is worth noting that the MPC retained the Articles of Religion from the MEC, going back to 1784, which speak at several points of "sacraments," but that elsewhere throughout the *Discipline*, from 1830 on, the MPC preferred to use instead the language of "ordinances," as in the duties of a superintendent just cited.

4 MPC *Discipline* 1830, 14.

authorized than that of elder."[5] Eligibility for election to ministerial office and ordination in the MPC was outlined as follows:

§10. Every preacher shall be eligible to deacon's orders, after he shall have preached two years under a license, and shall have arrived at the age of twenty-one years.

§11. Every deacon shall be eligible to elder's orders, when he shall have exercised the office of deacon acceptably two years.

§12. In cases of missions and similar necessities preachers may be elected to deacon's orders, and deacons to elder's orders, without regard to time, provided they possess the requisite qualifications.

§13. No person shall be elected to orders, except he be a man of unexceptionable moral character, genuine piety, respectable attainments, and sound in the belief of the fundamental doctrines of Christianity, and faithful in the discharge of gospel duties.[6]

And the authority of deacons and elders was described in these terms:

§14. The deacons shall have authority to preach the gospel, to baptize and celebrate matrimony, and to assist the elders in administering the Lord's Supper.

§15. The elders shall have authority to administer the Lord's Supper, baptize, celebrate matrimony, and perform all parts of divine worship.[7]

---

5   MPC *Discipline* 1830, 26.
6   MPC *Discipline* 1830, 45.
7   MPC *Discipline* 1830, 45–46.

There was no significant change in these disciplinary provisions until 1874. The MPC *Discipline* 1874 made no reference at all to deacons. According to Edward Drinkhouse, after previous unsuccessful efforts in 1850 and 1854 to abolish the order of deacons, at the 1874 General Conference of the MPC, "the order of deacons was stricken from the *Discipline*, with the form of ordination."[8] The language about authority of elders (p. 54) continued unchanged from 1830 until 1884, when the word "only" was added:

> §14. The elders *only* shall have authority to administer the Lord's Supper, baptize, and celebrate matrimony; but they shall not celebrate the marriage of divorced persons who have violated their marriage vows.[9]

Except for minor rephrasing, this language about the authority of elders was unchanged until 1900. In that year, the MPC, for the first time, granted sacramental authority to unordained preachers, via license from Annual Conference, to be annually renewed:

> §15. No itinerant preacher shall be eligible to ordination as an elder until he shall have preached three years under the appointment of an Annual Conference. But

---

8 See Edward J. Drinkhouse, *History of Methodist Reform Synoptical of General Methodism 1703 to 1898, With Special and Comprehensive Reference to its Most Salient Exhibition in the History of the Methodist Protestant Church*, 2 vols. (Baltimore: Board of Publication of the Methodist Protestant Church, 1899), 2:526; cf. 2:367 and 2:393. Drinkhouse notes that efforts to abolish the office of deacon in the MPC had begun as early as 1833 when the Tennessee Conference proposed that action (2:291), followed by the Boston Conference in 1838 (2:305).

9 MPC *Discipline* 1884, 71, italics added.

where it is necessary to provide for the administration of the ordinances in pastoral charges that cannot be supplied with elders, an Annual Conference may license the pastors of such charges to administer the ordinances, which license, when authorized by a vote of the Annual Conference and signed by the president and secretary, shall convey the same authority as ordination, except that it must be renewed annually. *Provided*, that is the candidate for ordination does not pass the studies of his year in the course of study, his license shall not be granted the following year. Unstationed preachers who have reached three years under a license, one year of which shall have been as a licentiate in this church, may, by a vote of the Annual Conference, be licensed to administer the ordinances; and after they have administered the ordinances for three years under a license they may be elected to orders. . . .

§18. Only elders and those who have been licensed to administer the ordinances shall have authority to administer the Lord's Supper, to baptize, and to celebrate matrimony; but they shall not celebrate the marriage of divorced persons who have violated their marriage vows.[10]

This language was unchanged in successive MPC *Disciplines* until 1916, when §15 was revised to allow seminary graduates to be ordained without passing the usual course of study and without a period of probationary service:

§15. No itinerant preacher shall be eligible to ordination as an elder until he shall have preached three years

___
10 MPC *Discipline* 1900, 76; MPC/JGC 1900, 123–24.

under the appointment of an Annual Conference. *Provided that any graduate of an approved Theological Seminary of the Methodist Protestant Church may be eligible to ordination without pursuing the Conference Course of Study or passing through a period of probation. . . .*[11]

The "seminary rule" of §15 (1916) may have been an attempt to ensure the enrollment of MPC ordination candidates at Westminster Theological Seminary, which was at the time the only seminary of the MPC. The rule was broadened in 1928 to extend to "an accredited theological seminary of an evangelical denomination"[12] but was otherwise unchanged, and there was no change in §18. After this, the language about sacramental authority in the MPC *Discipline* was unchanged until 1939.

---

11 MPC *Discipline* 1916, 51–52, italics added.
12 MPC *Discipline* 1928, 56.

The Methodist
Episcopal Church,
South
(1846–1939)

After its formal separation from the Methodist Episcopal Church in 1844, the Methodist Episcopal Church, South (MECS) held its first General Conference in 1846. There the MECS basically "cloned" the MEC *Discipline* of 1844, including the threefold ministry of bishops, elders, and deacons, and adopted the language about the sacramental authority of deacons and elders that was used by the MEC:

> Section VI: Of the Election and Ordination of traveling Elders, and of their Duty.
>
> *Quest.* 1. How is an elder constituted?
>
> *Ans.* By the election of a majority of the Annual Conference, and the laying on of hands of a Bishop, and of some of the elders that are present.
>
> *Quest.* 2. What is the duty of a traveling elder?
>
> *Ans.* 1. To administer baptism and the Lord's Supper, and to perform the office of matrimony, and all parts of divine worship.
>
> 2. To do all the duties of a traveling preacher. . . .

Section VII: Of the Election and Ordination of traveling Deacons, and of their Duty.

Quest. 1. How is a traveling deacon constituted?

Ans. By the election of the majority of the Annual Conference, and the laying on of hands of a Bishop.

Quest. 2. What is the duty of a traveling deacon?

Ans. 1. To baptize, and perform the office of matrimony, in the absence of an elder.

2. To assist the elder in administering the Lord's Supper.

3. To do all the duties of a traveling preacher. . . .[1]

There was some textual revision but no significant change in the language concerning the sacramental authority of deacons or elders in MECS *Disciplines* through 1906. In that year, a proposal came to the General Conference to revise the section specifying the duties of unordained preachers in charge of circuits, stations, or missions; for the first time authorizing them to administer the sacraments and to perform marriage services under certain conditions.[2] The debate about this proposal, as recorded in the *Daily Christian Advocate*, was vigorous:

James Cannon, Jr. (Virginia): My first charge was a large circuit of six Churches, and I had occasion to feel the great deprivation that came to my people because I was not able to do these things [baptize and administer the Lord's Supper] . . . by careful investigation

---

1 MECS *Discipline* 1846, (deacons) p. 51; (elders) p. 52; compare with MEC *Discipline* 1844, (elders) p. 34; (deacons) p. 35.

2 See P. A. Peterson, *History of the Revisions of the Discipline of the Methodist Episcopal Church, South* (Nashville: Publishing House of the M.E. Church, South, 1889).

I found that for sixty miles there was not a single Methodist preacher who could administer the rite of baptism or administer the sacrament of the Lord's Supper. . . . The consequence was that the statistics showed that through all that territory infant baptism had virtually passed away among us. We had no way to reach our people. The presiding elder came around four times a year, and once a year, perhaps, to the leading churches. . . . once a year would there be an opportunity to administer the rite of infant baptism to the children of my circuit. . . . What harm would we do should we give preachers in charge the right to baptize and celebrate the rite of matrimony, which is as far as the majority report goes. . . . Whenever we send a young man to any charge we ought to give him the full power to do the work of the ministry.

C. H. Briggs (Southwest Missouri): There are two ways in which the difficulty has been noted by the speaker who preceded me—and I recognize there is force in it—and two ways in which it is proposed to meet it. One is by authorizing all men appointed as preachers in charge to administer baptism and celebrate the rite of matrimony, even when unordained. The objection to that is that we discount our own ceremony of ordination. Ordination means something, or it means nothing. If there is any meaning in that solemn ceremony, we discount it and depreciate it when we commit its functions to men who have not been ordained. The other way of meeting the matter proposed in some of these memorials, but not approved by the committee, is to provide for the ordination of every man to the office of deacon when he is appointed a preacher in charge. That would virtually do away with probation for our ministers. There is this essential difference between licensing and ordaining a man—a man licensed receives authority for one year; at the end of that year the authority ceases, unless it is renewed. Ordination is permanent. I think the experience of these brethren shows the need of probation.

W. F. Tillett (Tennessee): We inherit a system that comes from conditions that were very different from what they are today. When our present system with reference to the prerogative of a preacher in charge who is unordained began, it was at a time when Methodism was compelled to put many a novice into the ministry. Young men were licensed to preach, and within a few weeks they were put in charge of Churches. . . . There was some reason . . . why there should be placed all necessary limitations upon their ministry. Those conditions have changed. We do not put the novice in charge of a Church. Our present system is, passing a young man through years of probation; and it is an exceedingly rare case that a young minister is put in charge who has not been on probation . . . he has been tried and tested. . . . I do not consider that administering the sacraments of baptism and the Lord's Supper is any more serious or sacred a function of his holy ministry than preaching the gospel.

Gross Alexander (Louisville): In the country young preachers are put in charge of circuits that are part of a large and extensive district, and they have perhaps protracted services, revival meetings, in which scores, or possibly hundreds, of people are converted, and they wish to join the Church. But the pastor of the Church, the man who has been the means of bringing these people to repentance and to Jesus Christ; who has been the means of conveying to them the truth that has resulted in their regeneration and salvation—this pastor is effectively estopped. . . . We say his people must stand outside the door and wait for one month, for two months, or three months, until some official who has been authorized to perform the act, which will admit them to the Church, shall come around. And meanwhile our young converts are losing their interest in the new life. . . . And our great founder, Mr. Wesley himself, in this very matter yielded to the demands of expediency. Do we not all recall, who know the history, that when necessity demanded it he waived those high-Church scruples of his which up to that time had been so dominant in his mind and life and usage? We are following a mighty good example when we follow the example of John Wesley.[3]

After amendment to substitute "baptism" for "the sacraments" (thereby excluding authorization for administration of the Lord's Supper), the proposal passed by a small margin (JGC/MECS 1906, pp. 97–99), and the following language was added to the paragraph of MECS *Discipline* 1906 describing the duties of a pastor in charge:

¶120. *Ans. 1.* To preach the gospel; to celebrate the rite of matrimony, provided it does not conflict with civil laws; in the absence of an Elder or Bishop, to administer baptism; and in the absence of the Presiding Elder or Bishop, to control the appointment of all services to

---

3   MECS/DCA 1906, pp. 35–37.

be held in the churches in his charge, *with the understanding that no permanent powers of ordination are conferred until the same shall be granted by the laying on of hands after he shall have met all the disciplinary requirements.*[4]

In their episcopal address to the 1910 General Conference, the MECS Bishops recommended repeal of the action taken by the 1906 General Conference:

> The change made by the last General Conference in paragraph 120, permitting any unordained preacher in charge of a station, circuit, or mission to [baptize and] celebrate the rite of matrimony, provided it does not conflict with civil laws, has yielded few practical benefits, has led to abuses and lowered the grade of our ordained ministry, and we recommend that the action then taken be repealed.[5]

This recommendation was referred to the Committee on Itinerancy, which did not recommend repeal of the 1906 action but, instead, the addition of a new sentence at the end of the paragraph (MECS/JGC 1910, pp. 342, 345). After debate, this change was incorporated into the *Discipline*: "Unordained preachers in charge shall have authority to celebrate the rite of matrimony only within their own pastoral charges."[6] There was no textual change in the paragraphs about deacons (¶¶155–57, p. 82) or elders (¶¶161–62, p. 84).

The MECS Bishops returned to the issue in their Episcopal Address to the subsequent General Conference in 1914:

---

4   MECS *Discipline* 1906, ¶120, pp. 58–59, italics added.
5   MECS/JGC 1910, 49.
6   MECS *Discipline* 1910, ¶123, p. 71.

A Question of Orders.—The change in our law made by the General Conference of 1906 and continued by the General Conference of 1910, whereby an unordained preacher in charge of a station, circuit or mission is permitted to celebrate the rite of matrimony, provided the civil law does not prohibit his doing so, and to administer baptism in the absence of an elder or bishop, has resulted in little practical good and has led to no little confusion. Your General Superintendents drew the attention of the General Conference of 1910 to the unwisdom of the law as it now stands, and we now ask your consideration for its repeal. We trust we shall not be regarded as impertinent if we set forth some of the reasons which lead us to the opinion held by us concerning it. In its present form the law reverses our historic position on the subject of ministerial orders and makes us peculiar among the Churches who have regard for any ordination at all. The only reason for Mr. Wesley's setting apart Dr. Coke for the mission upon which the latter was sent to America was to ordain men to administer the sacraments to the people who had long been without the ordinances. There were then men who argued as do the advocates of this law now; but Asbury firmly resisted them, and Mr. Wesley gave no countenance to their views. What light have we received justifying us in reversing the position of our Methodist fathers who founded our Church?

Moreover, this law is illogical in its conception, as well as confusing in its operation. It places the sacrament of the Lord's Supper upon a different and higher basis than that of the ordinance of baptism. This seems to be a novel view of the subject of orders. In some

Churches only a bishop can confirm candidates for Church membership; but with us, as the case now stands, any licentiate may, under certain circumstances, administer baptism, while a man must be an ordained elder to celebrate the Lord's Supper. . . .

No benefit that has ever been publicly alleged as arising from this law is sufficient to offset these and other weighty objections to it. With ordained men as presiding elders, visiting every pastoral charge once in three months at least, there seems to be no just reason for committing to unordained men these functions and thereby destroying, in a measure, the probationary method by which we try men who seek entrance into the ministerial office and conform to the apostolic exhortation to "lay hands suddenly on no man."[7]

Despite this impassioned protest from the Bishops, the 1906 legislation, as amended in 1910, was not changed by the 1914 General Conference. Eight years later, the 1922 MECS General Conference debated a report from the Committee on Itinerancy recommending that ¶142 of the *Discipline* be revised by inserting the words "and the sacrament of the Lord's Supper," thus enlarging the powers of preachers in charge who are unordained. The revised paragraph would read:

Question. What are the duties of preacher who has the charge of a circuit, station, or mission?

Answer 1. To preach the gospel (¶¶677, 680, and 681), to celebrate the rite of matrimony, provided it does not conflict with civic laws, in the absence of an elder or bishop to administer baptism and the sacrament of the

---

7   MECS/JGC 1914, 58–59.

Lord's Supper with the understanding that no permanent powers of ordination are conferred until the same shall be granted by the laying on of hands after he shall have met the disciplinary requirements, and in the absence of the presiding elder or bishop to control the appointment of all services to be held in the Churches in his charge. (718) Unordained preachers in charge shall have authority to celebrate the rite of matrimony only within their own pastoral charge, provided it does not conflict with civil laws.[8]

The majority report of the committee recommended nonconcurrence with this proposal; a minority report recommended concurrence. The debate on the floor of the General Conference was protracted and intense, bordering on hostility at points.

W. P. King (North Georgia): We hold no rigid theory of orders. The New Testament holds there are two. Mr. Wesley claims there are two orders. . . . We respect and will maintain our orders. But . . . it has always been the genius of Methodism . . . to make preeminent and supreme the call of human need, and to modify Church polity to conform to the need of humanity. . . . You say there is no need for any modification today. But in one of the oldest districts in the Church, a district of twenty-six charges and ninety-six Churches and a membership of eleven thousand, there were thirteen charges and forty-nine Churches, with a constituency of about 5,500, who did not receive the Lord's Supper except on occasion of the visit of the presiding elder.

---

8   MECS/DCA 1922, 57.

C. R. Jenkins (South Georgia): I have two thousand people under my charge. I go, day and night, over a large expanse of the best section of my State, and yet, to save my life, I cannot administer the sacrament to these two thousand people more than once a year. The young men who are pastors—college men—have no chance to be in the fullest sense the pastors of their people [because they cannot administer the sacraments to them].

J. H. Light (Baltimore): When I was elected to membership in this body I thought I was elected to membership in the General Conference of the Methodist Episcopal Church, South. I am not quite sure whether I am a member of the Southern Baptist Convention or in a congregation of the followers of Alexander Campbell. The genius of immersion in both of these great bodies . . . is the elevation of the right of baptism to a place of primacy among the sacraments of the Church. It means the subordination of the Lord's Supper to the rite of baptism. . . . The question before you this morning is whether you shall maintain the primacy of the sacrament of the Lord's Supper or whether you shall elevate the rite of baptism to that supreme position. . . . Among the men who shall be intrusted [*sic*] with this ministry there will be men [who are not] of sufficient maturity in Christian experience, in ministerial ability . . . to meet their people at the altar and lead them into the experience of the real sanctification of this great sacrament.

W. F. Bryan (Texas): There is nothing more sacred, to my mind, than the Word of God, and yet we send out young men to preach the gospel, to interpret the

Scriptures, who have not been ordained. There is nothing, in my mind, more sacred than the care of human souls, yet these men do go out and try to lead men and save them from sin. Now the speaker just gone before has declared to you the fact of the sacrament being such a tremendous means of grace. I believe that it is and for that very reason I believe that we ought to allow these young men to administer the sacrament of the Lord's Supper. . . . We have already allowed them to perform the marriage ceremony and administer baptism. If we will go a step farther now and allow them the privilege of administering the sacrament of the Lord's Supper, we will put them all on an even footing, in those rural sections, with our rival denominations.

W. A. Covington (South Georgia): Now, brethren, let's find out what we propose to do. We have 7,842 active preachers in our Church, and all of them are ordained except 467. In other words, 7,400 of them, in round numbers, are already ordained. Now, this movement proposes to confer upon these 467, scattered from Richmond to Mexico, in Europe, Asia, Africa, and the islands of the sea, the right to administer the sacrament of the Lord's Supper. . . . As I understand it, until about twelve years ago [actually, sixteen] no one but an ordained minister could administer the rite of baptism, or could marry people, or could administer the Lord's Supper. The change was made [in 1906] allowing the ministers not ordained to baptize people and marry people, and our brethren this morning seem to want to abolish an inconsistency, as they term it, to make people who are already eligible to baptize and marry eligible to administer the sacrament of the Lord's

Supper. Well, I don't think that the change should ever have been made. I don't believe that any minister other than an ordained minister of our Church should be even allowed to baptize people or marry people.

James A. Anderson (North Arkansas): This whole clamor for putting the privilege of administering the sacrament of the Lord's Supper into the hands of unordained men rests upon a false notion of sacramentarianism. . . . I would call attention to the fact that in the early days of Methodism there raged for years controversy in the Church about this very matter, whether we should proceed to ordain our American preachers. . . . Mr. Wesley, finally yielding, sent Dr. Coke to this country to make provision for that very thing, as well as to organize the Church. But . . . when they had organized the Church and proceeded to ordain men they had really relatively fewer elders then than we have today, yet the Church carried on its business. I would rather the sacrament should be administered once a year with due solemnity and gravity than that it should be administered every month in a slovenly manner.

M. T. Pyler (North Carolina): There is a difference between the priestly function and the prophetic message. Christ was both prophet and priest. There is no one in this Conference who will go beyond me in urging that the one need of this day and generation is a prophetic message that comes burning from the throne of God through the hearts of men prepared to speak for God. But notwithstanding that fact, I am here to say that we are not going to lay on the table the priestly function. . . . I plead that we stand with the genius and history of Methodism, that we keep some few things sacred and some places holy, and lay stress upon the man who is separated and set apart and comes down out of the mount with a shining face and a sense of the divine and of the sacrament of God because he has tasted, and is willing to have others have, a strange sense of the presence of the divine.

W. A. Tarver (Texas): The figures quoted by Dr. Covington must undoubtedly include all ordained deacons as well as ordained elders. Whether that is right or not, I do know upon reliable information that there are eleven hundred supplies trying to fill the waste places of Southern Methodism and to keep the pulpits of the Southern Methodist Church open in these rural communities. We have said to these supplies and to these unordained preachers, including the ordained deacons: "You can offer the people who come into the Church the experience of coming through the experience of the new birth, and thereby finding entrance into the Kingdom of God." Shall we say: "But you cannot administer the sacrament of the Lord's Supper"? Let us never come to the point where we shall exalt mere orders, mere words, mere forms above the needs of dying men and women in a broken-hearted and sin-cursed world.

J. P. Hilburn (Florida): I have traveled districts covering sections of the rural parts of the country and I have never yet found a place where it was not possible for me, as presiding elder, to arrange so as to supply the people with the sacrament of the Lord's Supper. . . . I am sure that the need is not so great now as it was in the days of Asbury, McKendree, Soule, and others who insisted that the ordination of our deacons and elders should not be a farce, but should mean something; and so, in this day of automobiles and good roads, and other means of transportation, there isn't the need for this legislation suggested by the minority as many of our brethren would have you believe. Shall we say that our fathers were unwise in all they did, standing as they have through almost a century and a half? Shall we discount their wisdom? Shall we be guilty of such rash legislation as to practically repudiate the history of our Church for almost a century and a quarter? I think we are not ready to take such a step today. . . . What will it mean when a man comes up to be consecrated elder . . . and the bishop shall place his hands on his head and give him the authority to exercise the office of an elder in the Church of God, and he turns and says, "For twenty years I have been doing all that," and no authority is granted and the ordination service is a mere farce?[9]

When the question was finally called, the minority report lost by the very slim margin of 8 votes, 170 to 178; the majority report was then adopted by a vote of 188 to 115, so no change was made in the *Discipline* (MECS/JGC 1922, pp. 103–105).

Exactly the same proposal came back to the 1926 General Conference, where again the majority report of the Committee on Itinerancy recommended nonconcurrence with the proposal, and a minority report recommended concurrence. The debate touched on familiar themes:

W. P. King (North Georgia): You remember very well this question came up at the Hot Springs General

---

9   MECS/DCA 1922, 58–60.

Conference [1922], when it was only defeated by a bare margin of five votes [actually 8 votes]. You remember that at that time it was defeated on the ground and through the appeal that this sacrament was of superior sanctity to the sacrament of baptism, thus separating the two sacraments insofar as their sanctity is concerned. In reply to the appeal that won out by a narrow margin at Hot Springs, I wish to quote from the Episcopal Address of 1914 which says that "this law is illogical in its conception as well as confusing in its operation. It places the sacrament of the Lord's Supper upon a different and higher basis than the ordinance of baptism. This seems to be a novel view of the subject of orders. In some churches only the Bishop can confirm candidates for membership, but with us any licentiate may under certain circumstances administer baptism, while a man must be ordained an Elder to celebrate the Lord's Supper." So the Episcopal Address of 1914 stands against the position that there is any difference in the sanctity of these two sacraments. And they are justified, because there is no shadow of anything in the New Testament that differentiates these two sacraments as touching their sanctity.

W. A. Cooper (Florida): I move to substitute for the whole that the law be so changed as to ordain a man a deacon when he is admitted on trial into the Annual Conference, and an Elder when he is admitted into full connection. . . . The present law in our Church was made when there were no schools and colleges. When a man came into the ministry he was made a junior preacher on a circuit and the senior preacher went around the circuit and performed these sacred acts.

But now it is altogether different. A young man comes to us and we know him and he is prepared, and why should we not keep our orders? Why, my brethren, have we made the ordination of deacons to be ridiculous in the Church? We have given to young men the right to perform certain duties as preachers in charge and yet when it comes to ordination the Bishop says to him, "Take thou authority to do some things." I ask you, if our ordination is the authority for doing these certain things, how can that young man do these things before he is ordained? [This motion was tabled.]

F. S. Onderdonk (Texas Mexican Mission): I do not think this is so much a solemn question as a practical question. In the mission over which I have the superintendency, about a thousand miles long by five hundred wide, the majority of my preachers are supplies or unordained men. It is impossible with these 30 pastoral charges for me to make four rounds a year to all those places, so that it comes to pass sometimes that our congregations go for six months without the sacrament of the Lord's Supper. We have one entire country where there is only one Protestant Church, and that is a Methodist Church. Our pastor in that community is an unordained man and therefore the sacrament of the Lord's Supper cannot be administered by a Methodist preacher in the whole country except as he breaks the law, which he at times does, for the reason that our Mexican people believe in the sacrament of the Lord's Supper. It is possible that there may be a little trace of the fanaticism of Romanism in it, but it does not destroy the fact that the sacrament of the Lord's Supper is to them a very precious thing. . . . It is a very serious matter when a man called upon to administer the sacraments under conditions like that has got to tell the people, "My Church sends me out to preach the Gospel but they will not allow me to administer a symbol of the Gospel!" . . . Let us be practical and give our man a chance to get out and do God's work.

B. F. Lipscomb (Virginia): He [Dr. Onderdonk] wants us to legislate for exceptional cases. We are here making laws for two and a half million Methodists and he wants us to make a law that will apply to this two and a half million Methodists because in a few fields, namely, mission fields, a certain condition exists. I submit that we cannot legislate in that fashion. We must legislate for the majority. And in the next place, this legislation is unnecessary. We have comparatively small districts in most of our charges. We cannot have more than 40, in most cases have not more than 25 to 30 [churches]. The Presiding Elder goes around the district four times a year and he, of course, is always authorized, and I suppose does, administer the sacrament wherever practical. In my district I have made a rule to have the sacrament administered either at the Quarterly Conference where we frequently have large gatherings of people on Saturday, or if not then, at the Church on Sunday. And so the Presiding Elder guarantees that the sacrament shall be administered at least four times a year. . . . If we had thoroughly prepared men such as were pictured in the eloquent address of my brother, Dr. Cooper, this argument might not have much force. But we have men in charge who are utterly unprepared to discharge all the duties of a preacher in charge. . . . There is something sacred about the administration of the sacrament. Our people have a feeling of reverence for [it]. . . . Our ritual is impressive and it needs a certain preparation in a man before he is prepared to administer the sacrament. To have a ritual mangled and mutilated as it is sometimes, or would be by men utterly unprepared by previous training of any sort to administer the sacrament, is a thing we ought to depreciate and not allow.[10]

In the end, the minority report was adopted, and the revised paragraph was incorporated in the MECS *Discipline* 1926 (after renumbering, ¶139, p. 77). This marked the point at which the MECS, for the first time, granted unordained preachers in charge of a circuit, station, or mission the right to administer the Lord's Supper. The MPC had made this move in 1900; the MEC never did so. This action by the 1926 General Conference thoroughly provoked the MECS Bishops, who spoke against it at length and in very strong language in their Episcopal Address to the 1930 General Conference:

A Question of Orders and Order.—The orders of deacon and or elder are as old as the organized Christian Church. Already, within the New Testament period, the administrative offices of the Church took this form. And through the long history of the Church deacons and elders have functioned in the sacred affairs of worship and of service with special reference to the administration of the sacraments of the Church. John Wesley, whose genius for administration along with his passion for the New Testament evangel gave to the world the Methodist Church, while refusing to be

---

10 MECS/DCA 1926, pp. 98–100; cf. MECS/JGC 1926, pp. 216–17.

bound by ecclesiastical tradition not rooted in history, was nevertheless careful to see that when Methodism was organized in America it should be organized in harmony with the practice of historic Christianity. In early days in the American colonies there seemed at times to be compelling reason why Methodists should break away from this orderly way of doing things and, without ordination, give the holy sacraments to the scattered members of their societies who had long been without these means of grace. But the wisdom of constructive minds such as was Francis Asbury's prevailed, and organized Methodism with a dignified and orderly way of doing things was the outcome.

We ask you to consider whether or not our Church is to go forward in harmony with the usages of the Christian Church from the early centuries and in keeping with the methodical and impressive manner in which Episcopal Methodism has from the beginning done its work in America, or whether we are to break with the usage of the past and disregard the practice of our own Church from its very organization in this country.

Speaking frankly, the matter of orders in our Church seems to us to be in a chaotic condition. Our present position is both illogical and embarrassing. What we refer to is as follows: When the bishop [p. 383] sets apart to the office of deacon the candidate presented to him by the Annual Conference, he addresses him in the following language: "It appertaineth to the office of a deacon to assist the elder in divine service, and especially, when he administereth the holy communion, to help him in the distribution thereof, and to read and expound the Holy Scriptures; to instruct the youth; and in the absence of the elder to baptize." Now, as a matter of fact, the man about to be ordained a deacon has already been doing every one of these things. He has not only been reading and expounding the Holy Scriptures; he has been, without the presence of an elder, administering the Holy Sacrament and baptizing also. For, as is generally known, recent legislation by the General Conference has given to any man serving as preacher in charge the right to perform the marriage ceremony, to administer the Sacrament of the Lord's Supper, and to baptize. We thus stand before the world in an illogical, unhistoric, and anomalous position. By General Conference majority legislation we have, in effect, reversed our historic Methodist position and have made our formal ordination to be empty of any real significance. But aside from this, there is no good reason why a man licensed to preach last month, and put in charge of a circuit this month, and having had no sufficient training for the work of the ministry, should be given the right and have imposed upon him the solemn responsibility to officiate at marriages, administer the Sacrament of the Lord's Supper, as well as to baptize. Such practice tends to belittle the sanctity of the marriage ceremony, which needs to have thrown about it all the holy influences of the Church, and to make the Sacrament of the Lord's Supper, which is the holiest of all the services of the Church, so unimpressive and commonplace as to empty it of any real spiritual significance. And there is no need of thus putting these solemn services in the hands of untaught and inexperienced beginners. If there ever was a time for this, that time has long since passed. In all parts of the Church elders and deacons are available for these services. Nowhere within our connection is there such a dearth of regularly ordained men as would justify such disregard both of orders and of proper order in the work of the Church. We earnestly recommend that this unwise legislative enactment be rescinded.

But if it should still seem wise to you to allow young men to administer the sacraments of the Church immediately upon assuming the duties of a preacher in charge, we suggest that, in lieu of our present legislation, you might consider the wisdom of making eligible to deacon's orders upon their admission on trial such candidates as fully meet the educational requirements of our Church; and that such as have passed the course of study required for elder's orders, or have received a Bachelor of Divinity degree from one of our accredited Schools of Theology, be made eligible to elder's orders upon their [p. 384] admission into full connection at the end of two years on trial in an Annual Conference.[11]

There is no evidence that the 1930 General Conference took any action on this plea from the MECS Bishops. The Bishops returned to the issue once again in their Episcopal Address to the 1934 General Conference:

Twelve years ago [actually it was in 1926, so eight years] our General Conference, with good purpose but with great breach of fundamental principles, hastily passed a law that allows an unordained man who is in charge of a circuit, station, or mission to celebrate the rite of

---

11 MECS/JGC 1930, 382–84.

matrimony and to administer baptism and the sacrament of the Lord's Supper. This is not only contrary to the historic position of all Methodism, but it is utterly subversive of the spirit and the practice of the Christian Church. Our conception of orders allows us to recognize the validity of ordinations and orders under all churches; but in them all, whether there be one, two, or three ordinations, the ordination always takes place before the rights and powers under the order are exercised. Our Methodism has become a distressing exception. Four years ago we earnestly recommended that "this unwise legislative enactment be rescinded" and we now renew that recommendation with increased desire and emphasis.[12]

Once again, the MECS General Conference declined to act on this urgent plea from their Bishops, and there was no change in the provisions dealing with sacramental authority in the MECS *Disciplines* of 1934 or 1938.

---

12 MECS/JCG 1934, 373.

The Debate at the Uniting Conference (1939)

The three denominational bodies coming into the Uniting Conference in 1939 had different positions regarding ministerial orders and sacramental authority. The MEC and MECS had maintained the traditional threefold ministry of bishops, elders, and deacons. The MPC had eliminated both bishops and deacons, but understood that accepting the episcopacy and the diaconate as maintained by both the MEC and the MECS was essential to the union, so there was little debate about that issue. The MPC had granted limited sacramental authority to unordained pastors in 1900, and the MECS had done so in 1906 (baptism) and 1926 (the Lord's Supper). The MEC had granted unordained preachers the authority to baptize and to marry in 1912, but had never allowed them to administer the Lord's Supper. The report of the Committee on Ministry and Judicial Administration to the 1939 General Conference proposed that The Methodist Church should follow the pattern of the MPC and the MECS, producing a vigorous debate that touched on a wide range of issues. That debate is worth careful attention, as it reflects and/or anticipates virtually all of the issues related to sacramental authority that have subsequently plagued The Methodist Church and The United Methodist Church.[1]

J. M. Potts (MECS, Virginia), chairman of the subcommittee that prepared the report, introduced it to the 1939 General Conference with these words:

> In the Methodist Episcopal Church, South, and in the Methodist Protestant Church, they grant to an Accepted Supply, using the term that has been used by the Methodist Episcopal Church, the right to administer the Sacrament of the Lord's Supper in the bounds of his own charge. There are many churches and many pastors who have this privilege at the present time. To take it away from them would cause a great deal of difficulty. We are asking that this privilege be granted in The Methodist Church. (p. 407)

Thomas S. Brock (MEC, New Jersey) argued that the Committee's proposal marked "a very great departure from the usual custom of the Church of which I have been a minister for a number of years":

> We have granted the right of accepted supply preachers to perform marriages and to baptize when the civil law of that particular state grants that function, because the man is in charge of a church.[2] To come to the place now where we are willing to grant the privilege of administering the Lord's Supper to an accepted

---

1 The debate is recorded in some detail in MC/DCA 1939, 407–411. All page numbers referenced in the following quotations are from this document.

2 This refers to the action taken by the MEC General Conference in 1912.

supply preacher, when we have laid very great emphasis on the necessity of ordination, and its function in
the Church, seems to me to be a very great departure from what would be the ordinary position of the
Church. (pp. 407–408)

J. W. Moore (MECS, Virginia) rose to speak in favor of the
Committee's proposal:

This has been no new question in the Methodist Episcopal Church, South. Some years ago, I think about
twenty, they allowed the young unordained pastor to
have the right of administration of the Lord's Supper.
[At] the succeeding General Conference, the Bishops,
in their deliverance to the General Conference, asked
that that right be taken away from them. The General
Conference almost unanimously reenacted the legislation which they had enacted before.[3]

The reason for it was this: that the preacher in
charge has no more sacred function than that of
preaching, and if we give him the right to preach, we
should also grant him the right of administration of the
Lord's Supper. The General Conference thought that
was rather degrading to the ministry.

There are many pastoral charges, especially in
the South, where they are served almost entirely by
unordained men, and shall we deny to these good
simple people that right that brings them in such

---

3 These comments confuse the actions taken by the MECS General
Conference in 1906, renewed in 1910, to allow unordained preachers appointed to a circuit or charge to marry and baptize, with the
1926 decision to also allow them to administer the Lord's Supper.

close fellowship with their Lord, simply because their preacher has not been ordained? (p. 408)

Disston W. Jacobs (MEC, Wilmington) offered an amendment designed to ensure that sacramental authority would be extended only to unordained preachers serving as appointed pastors in a full-time capacity, not to students or to those serving on a part-time basis:

> This is a very great departure from the usage of the Methodist Episcopal Church, and while it is true that the Methodist Episcopal Church, South, formerly did give to all accepted supplies, as has been stated, the right to administer the Lord's Supper, I do believe that we ought to have some distinction here.
>
> Here is a man who is a student and who has not completed his course, and he is serving as an accepted supply. What impetus is there for that fellow to go on and secure his ordination if you give him the privilege, all the privileges that are granted to a regularly ordained minister? We ought to have some distinction here between these men who are fully ordained and the men who are not fully ordained, and I trust you will accept this amendment. (p. 408)

W. P. King (MECS, North Georgia) then spoke against the Jacobs amendment:

> As has been intimated, this question has been threshed out several times before in our own [MECS] General Conference. . . .
>
> The distinction that is made between the two sacraments involves . . . placing the priestly element above the prophetic element in the preacher's ministry. When

a preacher is in charge of a church and has the authority to preach and to exercise his prophetic office, then certainly he should have the authority to exercise what we may term the priestly functions. . . .

In our own Church when there was an effort made to take away baptism from the unordained preachers, it was claimed that it was such a very sacred thing that it should not belong to them. Finally, when it was granted to them, then the fight was made against allowing them the right to administer the Sacrament by claiming that that was a right that was superior in sanctity to the right of baptism. Then when the effort was made to take both functions from the [unordained] pastor, the contradictory statement was made that they were entirely equal in sanctity and should not be celebrated. (p. 408)

This provoked a response from *Daniel L. Marsh (MEC, New Jersey)* in support of the Jacobs amendment:

Members of the Conference, I am not a pastor. I am not thinking of it from a pastor's point of view. I am thinking of it wholly from the people's point of view. I want to plead for an exaltation of the pastor, for a magnifying of his office. Let us not make the line of demarcation so dim that nobody can see it. The part-time local supply may be doing something else during the week, just the ordinary common labor of the parish, and then on Sunday the people see him administer the sacrament of the Lord's Supper and the sacrament of baptism, and they cease to have their really sacred and solemn significance.

When you have the full-time supply, then you have a certain amount of control over him. He has to take the Conference Course of Study and he is supposed to be giving himself to the preparation for the regular ministry. If I were amending this—I am not going to do it—but if I were doing it, I would ask that only the fully ordained minister should be privileged to administer these sacraments. I am not asking for that; I am asking most earnestly for the acceptance of the pending amendment. (p. 409)

J. M. M. Gray (MEC, Detroit) then proposed a substitute amendment to strike from the original committee report the whole paragraph granting sacramental authority to unordained preachers, speaking for this proposal in strong terms:

Like Dr. Marsh, I believe thoroughly that only the completely ordained minister should have the administration of the sacraments.

. . . I believe that we ought here to re-emphasize something of the great mystery and imaginative sense of the Christian faith and those amazing fundamental, perhaps imponderable realities by which men live religiously. I suggest to you that the spectacle of a man himself only a layman administering the holy exercises of our Christian faith does not greatly impress the laity of the Church. They are hungry for the unseen; they are hungry to maintain that separated character of the ministry in the past; and the great preaching influences of the past, and the great Church influences of the past have grown not from the likeness of the laity and the ministry in the exercise of worship function, but in the separated quality of the ministry which made the laymen call him a man of God. (p. 409)

This aroused vigorous opposition from *Roy O. Hills (MEC, Wyoming State)*:

I have great respect for the judgment of Dr. Marsh and Dr. Gray, but I am sure that they are looking at this question from the viewpoint of one who comes from a metropolis where there is not necessarily any need of administering the sacrament by other than fully ordained ministers. Were they traveling the great sections of Wyoming or Utah or Montana and coming up against the practical problem, their attitude would doubtless be different.

Out on one of the circuits in the state of Wyoming we have a supply pastor. He is a diamond in the rough. He is a man who works with his hands through the week somewhat and the people way out in the stretches have said this about him: "He seems to love us and work with us."

His hands, I submit to you, are just as sacred as the hands of any man who never toils through the week.

I am reminded just now that the hands that were nailed to the cross were the hands of a carpenter and I am certainly against this amendment. (p. 409)

Then, perhaps surprisingly, *Nolan B. Harmon, Jr. (MECS, Baltimore)* spoke in support of the Gray amendment:

An argument has been made here that there is a difference between the minister, that is to say the preacher, and the priest. It was said we create preachers or prophets, as someone has said, in a moment by putting them in charge, but make them wait some-times before we allow them to administer the sacra-ment of the Lord's Supper. . . .

Would to God we could make prophets by letting them go before some committee that licenses them to preach. We simply say, "Let the boys go in." We believe they are called. We let them be on trial for a while. After they have been on trial the Church gives them, through ordination, the power to administer the sacraments. We should not hurry them to rush in and form our judgement because someone is starting and has not yet proved himself.

I have no doubt that holy men, good men, untrained men, are just as much priests in this capacity, as much prophets as anyone else, but it is wiser to wait. Let the men be tested and in time let the Church, through the service of ordination, put its book into their hand and give them the authority to administer the sacraments, so we will lead our people better and make a better minister.

As a Southern man, I belong to that group of the Southern Church who never believe in the free giving away of our sacred power. (p. 409)

Fred B. Noble (MEC, St. Johns River), a lay delegate, spoke next in opposition to the Gray amendment:

I think nearly everyone who has spoken on this has been a minister. I am a layman. It seems to me that the layman's standpoint has not been presented. The statement has been made about the minister being set apart. Well, the minister *is* set apart.

The time has passed when they are the ones who have the learning of the community. They are not of the rich because they have those who are richer in the congregation. They are not set apart because they are poor, because they have those who are more poor in the congregation.

Therefore, if they are set apart, they must be set apart by character and life. I do not see why the godly man who is giving only a part of his time breaking the bread of life from the pulpit should not be authorized to administer the elements of the sacrament in time of need.

I have not yet heard an argument that any one taking the sacrament from the hand that has toiled in the garden, from one who has worked in the mine, or the carpenter during the week day, will not be as exalted, receiving the high benefits he could have received from one who has passed the Course of Study. (p. 410)

Harold P. Sloan (MEC, New Jersey) was then recognized; his remarks were directed to the proposal in the original committee report rather than to the pending Gray amendment:

I have found my mind quite divided as this debate has moved along. From the standpoint of mere analytical thinking, I would go with Dr. King. But I am persuaded there is a mystical value here which we imperil our whole Church impact if we neglect. You cannot always exactly analyze the mystical.

The fact of the matter is, the people feel a peculiar sanctity and reverence connected with the Lord's Supper. They do feel it; they feel that at that point they are attaining a relationship that is more intimate than any other. Whether we can exactly analyze and justify that point of view, it nevertheless is there and it expresses itself in the continual tendency toward the sacerdotal. It was that point of view in the minds of the people that produced the sacerdotalism of the Roman Catholic Church in the first place.

If we take this attitude, we unquestionably will diminish our reverence in the administration of the Lord's Supper. We will diminish it; we will diminish its impact upon our people and we ought to do it with very great caution.

The fact of the matter is, if you pass this legislation, you make ordination in The Methodist Church practically valueless for, since the minister has every power without ordination, why be ordained? And since you are correcting the inequity between traveling preachers and accepted supplies, you will find another effect of your action is to diminish the number of men who will get the necessary education to be members of your conferences.

The whole tendency of this action is mistaken. (p. 410)

The question was then called on the Gray amendment, and the subcommittee chairman, *J. M. Potts*, was given the final word in this part of the debate:

I hope this substitute [the Gray amendment] will not prevail. Several years ago, before this legislation [the original committee report] was adopted in the Southern Methodist Church, I was as heartily opposed to it as those who have spoken against it today. However, in the last, now nearly four years, I have been the

Presiding Elder of the Richmond District in Virginia and have been observing its practice. As I have observed it, I cannot see that these fears developed in the practice. In fact, I favor it heartily, though I was opposed to it in the beginning.

There are ten supplies in the District which I serve, with ten churches—more than that because some of them are circuits—which come under this classification. To go back and tell them that our practice had been changed would cause many difficulties.

We debated this matter in the subcommittee at length. It was recommended to the Standing Committee. You will notice that the Standing Committee voted unanimously in favor of the provision to grant this right. Therefore, I am opposed to the substitute and hope the substitute will not prevail. (p. 410)

A vote was then taken, and the Gray amendment was defeated. This brought the earlier Jacobs amendment to the floor. After some procedural matters were handled, and following a request for clarification of the exact wording of the amendment, lay delegate *A. C. Bennett (MEC, Kentucky)* was recognized:

Listening to this discussion one would almost be forced to the conclusion that this sacrament was instituted solely for the benefit of the preachers. The discussion here has hinged almost entirely on the question of the right of the minister. I believe the sacrament was instituted for the benefit of the laymen as well as the minister. I know sections where members of churches have not had the opportunity to take the sacrament more than once a year, and I think in the interest of the laity this rule ought to be liberalized so that they might have the privilege of the sacrament. In addition, when the minister is given the privilege of administering this sacrament, it increases his influence in the community, among the membership. It will raise it very materially, if they understand that they have a pastor who will administer the sacrament. (p. 411)

The question was then called on the Jacobs amendment, and after some additional parliamentary procedures were cleared, a vote was taken and the amendment was defeated. The original committee report was then adopted, thereby extending sacramental authority in The Methodist Church to unordained preachers serving under appointment as pastors in charge.

The Methodist
Church
(1939–1968)

As a result of the decisions and actions of the 1939 General Conference, The Methodist Church (MC) at its formation adopted the position on sacramental authority that had been inaugurated by the MPC in 1900 (MPC *Discipline* 1900, "Government of the Church," §18, p. 76) and by the MECS in 1926 (MECS *Discipline* 1926, ¶139.1, p. 77). The MEC had never authorized unordained preachers to administer the Lord's Supper. The debate at the 1939 Uniting Conference led to the inclusion of the following provisions in the MC *Discipline* 1939:

(1) A pastor was defined as "a Preacher who, by appointment of the Bishop or District Superintendent, is in charge of a Station or Circuit." The duties of a Pastor were listed in twenty-six separate sections of ¶223, but the first duty listed concerned administration of the sacraments:

¶223.1. To preach the gospel; to perform the Marriage Ceremony, and to administer the Sacraments of Baptism and the Lord's Supper, according to the Discipline.[1]

---

1   MC *Discipline* 1939, ¶223, p. 68.

(2) Since the category of *pastor* could include both ordained and unordained individuals, the following provisions specifically conveyed limited sacramental authority to unordained pastors:

¶223.2.3 An unordained Pastor and a Local Preacher serving as an Accepted Supply shall have authority to perform the Marriage Ceremony, provided it is not in conflict with civil laws; and to administer the Sacrament of Baptism and the Lord's Supper in the bounds of his own Charge, in the absence of the District Superintendent, *with the understanding that no permanent powers of ordination are conferred until granted by the laying on of hands after he has met the Disciplinary requirements.*[2]

(3) The following paragraphs described the authority of deacons and elders respectively:

¶252. A Deacon has authority to preach; to conduct Divine Worship; to perform the Marriage Ceremony; to administer Baptism; and to assist an Elder in administering the Lord's Supper (¶223, Art. 2, subsection 3, shall apply).[3]

¶260. An Elder has authority to preach; to conduct Divine Worship; to administer the sacraments of Baptism and the Lord's Supper, and to perform the Marriage Ceremony.[4]

The MC *Discipline* 1940 made no textual change in the language about the authority of deacons (¶252, p. 83) or elders

---

2   MC *Discipline* 1939, ¶223.2.3, pp. 68–69, italics added.

3   MC *Discipline* 1939, ¶252, p. 81.

4   MC *Discipline* 1939, ¶260, p. 83.

(¶260, p. 85). The former section about "Pastors" was transferred into a new section headed "Local Preachers" within a new chapter titled "The Local Ministry." Unordained local preachers continued to be given authority for sacramental administration and performance of marriages under carefully specified conditions:

> ¶287. *Art.* 7. Unordained Local Preachers, only while serving as regularly appointed Pastors of Charges, shall be authorized to administer the sacraments of Baptism and the Lord's Supper, and, when the laws of the state permit, to perform the Marriage Ceremony; but in all Foreign Mission Fields, the conferring of such authority shall rest with the Central Conferences in which they are Pastors.[5]

There was no significant change in the MC *Discipline* 1944 in the language about the authority of deacons (¶393, pp. 108–109) or elders (¶402, p. 110). The paragraph granting sacramental authority to unordained pastors was significantly revised to require written authorization from the bishop, renewed annually:

> ¶352.2. The duties of a pastor are:
> 1. To preach the gospel.
> 2. To administer the Sacraments of Baptism and the Lord's Supper, to perform the marriage ceremony, and to bury the dead, according to the Discipline.
> An unordained pastor or a local preacher serving as an accepted supply may, upon recommendation by his district superintendent and written consent of the resident bishop, be authorized to administer the

---

5   MC *Discipline* 1940, ¶287, p. 90.

Sacraments of Baptism and the Lord's Supper and to perform the marriage ceremony, if the laws of the state permit. Any exercise by him of his authorization outside the bounds of his charge shall be sufficient cause for the revocation of his authorization by his bishop upon recommendation of his district superintendent. Written consent by the bishop shall be on a form prepared by The Methodist Publishing House and must be renewed annually. It is understood that no permanent powers of ordination are conferred until granted by the laying on of hands after he has met the Disciplinary requirements.[6]

No significant change was made in the language of the MC *Discipline* 1948 about the authority of deacons (¶393, p. 115) or elders (¶402, p. 116). A parenthetical statement was included in the paragraph about the sacramental authority of unordained pastors stating that "this provision shall be in effect until the General Conference of 1952."[7] The MC *Discipline* 1952 made no change in the language about the authority of elders.[8] The paragraph about the authority of deacons was expanded:

¶393. A deacon has authority to preach, to conduct divine worship; to perform the marriage ceremony, to administer Baptism, and to assist an elder in administering the Lord's Supper; *provided* that, while serving as a regularly appointed pastor of a charge, he may be

---

6   MC *Discipline* 1944, ¶352.2, p. 98; cf. ¶306, p. 88.

7   MC *Discipline* 1948, ¶352.2, p. 103.

8   MC *Discipline* 1952, ¶402, p. 130.

authorized to administer the Lord's Supper under the conditions set forth in ¶308.[9]

The paragraph concerning the sacramental authority of unordained pastors was significantly revised:

¶308. An unordained pastor, only while serving as a regularly appointed pastor of a charge, may be authorized to administer the Sacraments of Baptism and the Lord's Supper and, if the laws of the state permit, to perform the marriage ceremony, within the bounds of his pastoral charge, *provided:* (a) he has passed the course of study for admission on trial (¶2204), and, (b) each year thereafter he passes one full year of the course of study looking to full ordination. Failure to complete one full year annually shall cause suspension of this privilege. In foreign mission fields the conferring of such authority shall rest with the Central Conference in which the pastor serves. (For requirements for ordination see ¶¶392–404.)[10]

There was no significant textual change in the language about the authority of deacons (¶392, p. 139) or elders (¶402, p. 141) in the MC *Discipline* 1956. The language about the sacramental authority of unordained pastors was again revised, in part to reflect the elimination of the "Seminary Rule" (from 1924), which had mandated the Course of Study as the route to qualification for a pastoral appointment:

¶318.1. An unordained approved supply pastor, only while serving as a regularly appointed pastor of a charge, shall be authorized to administer the Sacraments

---

9   MC *Discipline* 1952, ¶393, p. 129, italics original.
10 MC *Discipline* 1952, ¶308, pp. 106–7, italics original.

of Baptism and the Lord's Supper and, if the laws of the state permit, to perform the marriage ceremony, within the bounds of the charge to which he is assigned; *provided* that: (a) he shall have passed the introductory studies for the ministry (¶¶1374, 2044); and (b) each succeeding year he shall be enrolled as a regular full-time student in a pretheological or theological course in a college, university, or school of theology accredited or approved by the University Senate, or by the state accrediting agency, or shall have passed one full year of the ministerial course of study looking to full ordination. Failure to complete one full year annually shall cause suspension of this privilege. In all missionary fields abroad the conferring of such authority shall rest with the Central Conference in which the pastor serves.

2. An unordained part-time approved supply pastor (¶317 §2) who completes each year two books of the ministerial course of study, and continues until he is graduated from the course, shall be authorized, while serving as a regularly appointed pastor of a charge, to administer the sacrament of Baptism and, if the laws of the state permit, to perform the marriage ceremony within the bounds of the charge to which he is assigned.[11]

In the MC *Discipline* 1960, the language about the authority of both deacons and elders was revised:

¶392. A deacon has authority to preach, to conduct divine worship, to perform the marriage ceremony, to

---

11 MC *Discipline* 1956, ¶318, pp. 119–20; cf. ¶352.2, p. 127, italics original.

administer Baptism, and to assist an elder in administering the Lord's Supper; *provided* that, while serving as a regularly appointed pastor of a charge, he shall be authorized to administer the Lord's Supper under the conditions set forth in ¶318; and *provided,* further, that a local preacher who is ordained deacon shall be authorized to exercise ministerial functions only in the charge to which he is appointed or in which he resides.

¶402. An elder has authority to preach, to conduct divine worship; to administer the sacraments of Baptism and the Lord's Supper, and to perform the marriage ceremony; *provided,* however, that a local preacher who is ordained elder shall be authorized to exercise ministerial functions only in the charge to which he is appointed or in which he resides.[12]

The language about the sacramental authority of unordained pastors was again revised:

¶318.1. An unordained approved supply pastor, only while serving as a regularly appointed pastor of a charge, may be permitted to administer the Sacraments of Baptism and the Lord's Supper and, if the laws of the state permit, to perform the marriage ceremony, within the bounds of the charge to which he is assigned; *provided* that: (a) he shall have completed one fourth of the work required for the bachelor of divinity or equivalent degree in a school of theology accredited or approved by the University Senate, or shall have passed the introductory studies for the ministry (¶1374); and (b) each

---

12 MC *Discipline* 1960, (deacons) ¶392, p. 152; (elders) ¶402, p. 153, italics original.

succeeding year he shall be enrolled as a regular full-time student in a pre-theological or theological course in a college, university, or school of theology accredited or approved by the University Senate, or by the state accrediting agency, or shall have passed one full year of the ministerial course of study looking to full ordination. Failure to complete one full year annually shall cause suspension of this privilege. Authorization must be given in writing by the resident bishop under whom he serves after approval by the Annual Conference. In all missionary fields abroad the conferring of such authority shall rest with the Central Conference in which the pastor serves.

2. An unordained part-time approved supply pastor (¶317.3) who completes each year two books of the ministerial course of study, and continues until he is graduated from the course, shall be authorized, while serving as a regularly appointed pastor of a charge, to administer the sacrament of Baptism and, if the laws of the state permit, to perform the marriage ceremony within the bounds of the charge to which he is assigned.[13]

There was no significant change in the MC *Discipline* 1964 in the language about the authority of deacons (¶392, p. 168), elders (¶402, p. 169), or the sacramental authority of unordained pastors (¶318, pp. 147–48).

---

13 MC *Discipline* 1960, ¶318, pp. 131–32; cf. ¶392, p. 152.

The Evangelical United Brethren Church (1946–1968)

The Evangelical United Brethren Church (EUBC) was formed in 1946, by merger of the Evangelical Church and the United Brethren Church; its first approved *Discipline* appeared in 1947. Ordained ministers had full sacramental authority by virtue of their ordination. Unordained ministers serving under appointment could be granted sacramental authority by the Annual Conference, such authority presumably being limited to the church or charge to which they were appointed:

¶367. An ordained minister is authorized to administer the sacraments of baptism and the Lord's Supper, and to solemnize marriage.

¶368. An unordained Minister who is regularly serving a Charge may, by special annual grant from the Annual Conference, be permitted to administer the sacraments. Where the laws of a State or Province permit a regularly licensed, but as yet, unordained Minister to solemnize marriage, Probationers regularly serving Charges may solemnize marriage.[1]

---

1   EUBC *Discipline* 1947, (ordained ministers) ¶367; (unordained ministers) ¶368, p. 122.

The EUBC made no changes in its language about sacramental authority until 1959, when the paragraph about sacramental authority for unordained ministers was revised but not significantly altered:

¶368. In cases of necessity, where it is impractical for the annual conference to make other satisfactory arrangements, an unordained minister who is regularly serving a charge may, by special grant from the annual conference in which he is serving, be permitted to administer the sacraments. Where the laws of a state or province permit a regularly licensed, but as yet unordained minister to solemnize marriage, probationers regularly serving charges may solemnize marriage.[2]

The EUBC made no further changes in this Disciplinary language through 1967.

---

2 EUBC *Discipline* 1959, ¶368, p. 90.

The United
Methodist Church
(1968–2016)

At its establishment in 1968, The United Methodist Church (UMC) faced the difficulty of reconciling the differing positions of The Methodist Church (1939–1968) and the Evangelical United Brethren Church (1946–1968) on a variety of matters. Their positions on sacramental authority for ministers were not radically dissimilar. The paragraphs of The UMC *Discipline* 1968, describing the authority of deacons and elders, read as follows:

> ¶311. *The Order of Deacon.*—A deacon is a minister who has been received by an Annual Conference either as a probationary member or as an associate member and has been ordained deacon. A deacon has authority to conduct divine worship, to preach the Word, to perform the marriage ceremony where the laws of the state or province permit, and to bury the dead. When invited to do so by an elder, he may assist in the administration of the Sacraments. When serving as a regularly appointed pastor in charge, he shall be granted authority to administer the Sacraments on the charge to which he is appointed.

¶313. *The Order of Elders.*—An elder is a minister who has met the requirements of ¶314 and therefore has full authority for the ministry of Word, Sacrament, and Order; who has been received as a minister in full connection with an Annual Conference; and who has been ordained elder (¶331–32).[1]

Unordained persons approved to perform pastoral duties were now called "lay pastors." The paragraphs of the *Discipline* describing the authority of lay pastors (¶¶338–49) contained this language:

> ¶338. *Lay Pastor.*—A lay pastor is a layman duly licensed to preach who upon recommendation of the Board of Ministry, has been approved by the ministerial members in full connection as eligible for appointment as pastor of a charge. He shall have authority within the bounds of the church to which he is appointed to perform the duties of a pastor as specified in ¶¶349–50. . . .
>
> ¶349.1. A lay pastor while serving under appointment as pastor of a charge shall be responsible to perform all the duties of a pastor (¶350) except that he shall not be authorized to administer the Sacraments. In performance of his pastoral duties he shall be under the supervision of the district superintendent and the guidance of a duly assigned counseling elder.[2]

There are several things worth noting here. First, deacons were authorized to administer the sacraments of baptism and the Lord's Supper "when serving as a regularly appointed

---

1 UMC *Discipline* 1968, (deacons) ¶311, p. 110; (elders) ¶313, p. 110.
2 UMC *Discipline* 1968, ¶338, p. 123; ¶349.1, p. 126.

pastor in charge." Second, unordained local pastors ("lay pastors") were prohibited from administering either baptism or the Lord's Supper, even when serving under appointment as pastor in charge; this constituted a significant change from pre-1968 positions of both the MC and the EUBC. Finally, all pastors under appointment, whether ordained or not, were authorized to perform marriages in the charges to which they were appointed (where state laws permitted).

The paragraph of The UMC *Discipline* 1972 describing the authority of deacons was revised so as to specifically include qualified lay pastors:

> ¶311. *The Order of Deacon.*—A deacon is a minister who has been received by an Annual Conference either as a probationary member or as an associate member or is a lay pastor who qualified in accordance with ¶312.1, and has been ordained deacon. Deacons have authority to conduct divine worship, to preach the Word, to perform the marriage ceremony where the laws of the state or province permit, and to bury the dead. When invited to do so by an elder, they may assist in the administration of the Sacraments. When serving as regularly appointed pastors in charge, they shall be granted authority to administer the Sacraments in the charge to which they are appointed.[3]

There was no textual change in the paragraph describing the authority of elders (¶313, p. 145). The paragraph specifying the authority of lay pastors was revised as follows:

> ¶349.1. Lay pastors, while serving under appointment as pastors of charges, shall perform all the duties of

---

3 UMC *Discipline* 1972, ¶311, p. 144.

pastors, except that if unordained they shall not be authorized to administer the Sacraments of Baptism and the Lord's Supper. Their continuing eligibility to be appointed shall be contingent upon annual fulfill-ment of the appropriate requirement of ¶348. Their authority to perform pastoral duties shall be limited to the charge to which they are appointed. In the performance of these duties, they shall be under the supervision and pastoral authority of the district super-intendent and the guidance of a duly assigned counsel-ing elder.[4]

There was no significant textual change in the section of the *Discipline* dealing with the "Duties of a Pastor" (¶350, pp. 163–65).

In a very significant change, the term *lay pastor* was replaced in The UMC *Discipline* 1976 by the term *local pastor.* This helped resolve the semantic confusion of the 1972 *Discipline* about the ordination status of the *lay pastor* in relation to the order of dea-cons. The authority of local pastors was described as follows:

¶408. *Requirements for a Local Pastor.*—1. A local pastor is a person certified by the district Commit-tee on Ordained Ministry for recommendation to the Board of Ordained Ministry to be approved by min-isterial members in full connection and to be autho-rized to perform all the duties of a pastor (¶453.2) including the Sacraments of Baptism and Holy Com-munion as well as the service of marriage (where state laws allow), burial, confirmation, and member-ship reception, while assigned to a particular charge

---

4   UMC *Discipline* 1972, ¶349.1, p. 162.

under the specific supervision of a counseling elder subject to annual renewal. Such authorization must be re-certified by the bishop when assignments change between sessions of the Annual Conference.[5]

Further, three different categories of local pastor were defined, each with a different set of qualifications and requirements: full-time (¶409.1, p. 172), part-time (¶409.2, p. 173), and student (¶409.4, pp. 173–74). That all of this represented a major change from the provisions of the *Disciplines* of 1968 and 1972 is demonstrated by a separate provision stipulating that "none of the provisions of this legislation shall be interpreted to change or limit authorizations to persons ordained as deacon and elder prior to 1976 or enrolled in the appropriate studies prior to January 1, 1977."[6] In addition, local pastors were now specifically authorized to perform baptisms and to administer Holy Communion "while assigned to a particular charge and under the specific supervision of a counseling elder subject to annual renewal."[7] This had the effect of restoring the sacramental authority that had been removed in 1968 from unordained preachers serving under appointment as local (or lay) pastors.

The paragraph outlining the authority of deacons was slightly revised in light of the foregoing, removing the previous reference to lay pastors as being deacons:

> ¶449. *The Order of Deacon.*—A deacon is a minister who has been received by an Annual Conference either as a probationary member or as an associate member has been ordained deacon. Deacons have authority to

---

5   UMC *Discipline* 1976, ¶408, p. 170.

6   UMC *Discipline* 1976, ¶409.5, p. 174.

7   UMC *Discipline* 1976, ¶408, p. 170.

conduct divine worship, to preach the Word, to perform the marriage ceremony where the laws of the state or province permit, and to bury the dead. When invited to do so by an elder, they may assist in the administration of the Sacraments. When serving as regularly appointed pastors of charges, they shall be granted authority to administer the Sacraments on the charges to which they are appointed.[8]

There was no significant change in the paragraph specifying the authority of elders (¶450, p. 204). The section of the *Discipline* dealing with the "Duties of a Pastor" (¶453.2, pp. 206–207) was revised and streamlined, and a new paragraph was added concerning "Appointment to a Pastoral Charge":

A pastor is an ordained or licensed person approved by vote of the ministerial members in full connection (¶¶408–409), appointed by the bishop to be in charge of a station, circuit, larger parish or on the staff of one such appointment.[9]

This covered those appointed to be associate pastors or to specialized ministries (such as children's minister or youth minister) in larger congregations.

There was no significant change in The UMC *Discipline* 1980 to the language of the paragraphs describing the authority of local pastors (¶408, p. 186), deacons (¶434, p. 209), or elders (¶435, p. 210). The paragraphs about the authority and duties of local pastors were revised in The UMC *Discipline* 1984:

¶406. *Authority and Duties.*—1. A local pastor is a person licensed by the district Committee on Ordained

---

8 UMC *Discipline* 1976, ¶449, p. 204.

9 UMC *Discipline* 1976, ¶453.1, p. 206.

Ministry to perform all the duties of a pastor (¶439) including the Sacraments of Baptism and Holy Communion as well as the service of marriage (where state laws allow), burial, confirmation, and membership reception, while assigned to a particular charge.

2. Such authorization granted by the license may be renewed annually by the district Committee on Ordained Ministry and extends only within the charge to which the local pastor is appointed.

3. The license shall remain valid only so long as the appointment continues and must be recertified by the bishop when assignments change between sessions of the Annual Conference.

4. A local pastor shall be under the supervision of a district superintendent and a counseling elder who shall supervise the local pastor's work in the ministerial course of study and give counsel on matters of pastoral responsibility.[10]

There was no significant change in the paragraph specifying the authority of deacons (¶433, p, 219) or elders (¶434, p. 220). The section of the *Discipline* formerly called "Duties of a Pastor" was renamed as "Ministering within the Congregation and to the World" and renumbered but not significantly changed (¶439, p. 223).

In The UMC *Discipline* 1988, a local pastor was defined as "a lay person approved annually by the district Committee on Ordained Ministry *and licensed by the bishop* to perform all the duties of a pastor (¶439) including the Sacraments of Baptism and Holy Communion as well as the service of marriage (where state laws allow), burial, confirmation, and membership

---

10 UMC *Discipline* 1984, ¶406, pp. 194–95.

reception, while assigned to a particular charge."[11] There was no significant modification of the nature of their authority or the conditions of their service. There was no change in the language of the paragraphs concerning the authority of deacons (¶434, p. 240) or elders (¶435, p. 241). The section of the *Discipline* on "Ministering within the Congregation and to the World" was set once more within the context of "Responsibilities and Duties of a Pastor" (¶439, pp. 244–45). There was no significant modification of the nature of the authority of pastors or the conditions of their service.

There were only minor textual changes in The UMC *Discipline* 1992 in the paragraphs concerning local pastors (¶406, p. 207), deacons (¶434, p. 233), elders (¶435, p. 234), and the "Responsibilities and Duties of a Pastor" (¶439, pp. 236–37). The language of the first paragraph about local pastors was slightly but significantly revised and expanded in The UMC *Discipline* 1996:

> ¶340. *Authority and Duties.*—1. A local pastor is approved annually by the district committee on ordained ministry and licensed by the bishop to perform the duties of a pastor (¶331), including the sacraments of baptism and Holy Communion as well as the service of marriage (where state laws allow), burial, confirmation, and membership reception, while appointed to a particular charge. Local pastors are not eligible for appointment beyond the local church. For the purposes of these paragraphs the charge will be defined as "people within or related to the community being served."[12]

11 UMC *Discipline* 1988, ¶406.1, p. 212, italics added.
12 UMC *Discipline* 1996, ¶340.1, p. 216.

There was no further significant modification of the nature of the authority or the conditions of the service of local pastors. However, there was dramatic modification in the language about the nature and authority of the ministry of the deacon. In what some observers described as the "Denver Revolution of 1996," The UMC abandoned over two hundred years of precedent and replaced the old system under which ordination as a deacon was a step toward ordination as an elder by making deacons and elders into two separate, distinct, but parallel orders of ministry. As John Harnish has put it,

> In 1996, the General Conference of The United Methodist Church reordered the ministry of the denomination in light of a growing understanding that all Christians are called to ministry, and a correlative understanding that ordained ministry is primarily charged with leading others to find a place for themselves in the ministry that all Christians share. In that reordering, probably the most far-reaching change was the creation of a new order of deacon—an ordained person, a full member of the Annual Conference, non-itinerant, and called to a lifetime of ministry relating the gathered life of the community to servant ministry in the world.[13]

This came about as a legislative proposal from the Council of Bishops, developed after a ministry study by the Council, during the 1992–1996 quadrennium, when it was referred to the 1996 General Conference's Ministry Study Committee. The original recommendation of the Bishops had been that all candidates for ordination, whether as deacon or as elder, be ordained first as deacons, with ordination as elders being a

---

13 Harnish, *The Orders of Ministry in The United Methodist Church*, 110–11.

second, subsequent service for those called and approved for membership in that order. By a very large margin (92–12), the legislative committee recommended that there be only one, separate ordination for each order. When this was presented to the General Conference, the floor debate was vigorous.[14]

J. Lawrence McCleskey (Western North Carolina) immediately moved the substitution of the original proposal from the Council of Bishops for the legislation proposed by the committee:

> I support the new deacon as proposed both in the bishops' study and the report of the legislative committee. My concern is with the effect of the legislative committee's proposal on the elder. The committee proposes two ordinations to either deacon or elder separately. The bishops' proposal places ordination as deacon in a much more central place in the understanding of ordination. By providing that all ordained persons be first ordained deacons, the bishops' proposal affirms the deacon's ordination to service as the foundation of all ordination in our church. If we adopt the proposal of the committee, we will depart from almost 1700 years of tradition which has characterized most of Christendom, including the Anglo-Catholic tradition out of which Wesley came, as well as the mainstream of American Methodism since Francis Asbury. The sequential pattern of ordination, first as a deacon and then, for those called, as an elder began to be required in the church in the early fourth century . . . most of Christendom for 1700 years and most of Methodism

---

14 UMC/DCA 1996, vol. 3, pp. 693–700. All page numbers referenced in the following quotations are from this document.

for over 200 years has followed this sequential pattern for ordination, thus grounding all ordination in a servant ministry. (pp. 696–97)

Mary Elizabeth Moore (California-Pacific) spoke in support of the legislative committee's report in terms that challenged the historical framing of the issue by McCleskey, preferring to cast it as looking forward to the future rather than backward to the past:

I think the question before us tonight is the question of where are we going, and where is God calling us into this future? . . . What the bishops have done, in the document they've offered, is to challenge us to realize that in our baptism we are incorporated into the Body of Christ. We are incorporated into a servant ministry and that is the base of all ministry. The base of our ministry is in baptism not in the diaconate. . . . If the ministry of the Christian church is grounded in baptism, then the servanthood of all Christians is the ground from which all ministry comes. We don't therefore need to be ordained first as deacons. (p. 697)

After comments from *Helmut Nausner (Austria)* supporting the McCleskey substitute and from *Suzi Robertson (Texas)* and *Armin Besserer (Germany)* opposing it, *George Atkinson (Texas)* was recognized:

I don't know that it would make any difference to my congregation if we kept the present order of the *Discipline*, or adopted the bishops' proposal, or took the legislative committee's proposal. Most congregations want caring pastors who are able to preach and people who will help them grow in the Christian life.

But I can't help but think that changing the way we've done things for so long, that will take so much energy over the next several years to work out, is not the best way to perfect the order of deacon. Certainly we need to work on creating a permanent deacon, a deacon who has a particular work in the world, who is able to embody and witness to the Word, but I don't see that doing that requires that we alter the way we think about elders.

The grounding of ministry is not simply in baptism. There is only one ministry—that's the ministry of Jesus Christ. Baptism allows us to participate in that ministry. The ministry of Jesus Christ is described by many theologians as being that of prophetic, priestly, and royal work, which is why we have reflected in our own ordination Word and Sacrament and Order. . . . There are not conflicting and separated orders of deacon and elder, not to mention whatever bishops are. (p. 698)

W. Earl Bledsoe, the chair of the legislative subcommittee, was then recognized to give the last word from the committee.

We affirm the ministry of all persons, both laity, deacons and elders working together in ministry. . . . [W]hen we look at the model which we put forth in the amended version of the bishops' study, we find it has clarity. And it has focus on the ministry of servanthood. . . . It clears up the perception among those who are in ministry within the church that this is a hierarchy, or that some are more superior, or inferior, to others in our ministry. We should be about the ministry of Jesus Christ in service to all persons, and we ought to be able to utilize the gifts that everyone brings to the table to share the gospel of Jesus Christ to others. (pp. 698–99)

A vote was then taken on the McCleskey substitute, which lost by a vote of yes, 224; no, 710. This put the original committee report back on the floor. A good deal of additional discussion followed, further amendments were introduced and tabled or defeated, and finally the proposal of the legislative committee was approved with 769 affirmative votes. Consequently, this language appeared in The UMC *Discipline* 1996:

¶311. *Order of Deacons and Order of Elders.*—There shall be in each annual conference an Order of Deacons and an Order of Elders. All persons ordained as clergy in The United Methodist Church upon election to full membership in the annual conference shall be members of and participate in an Order appropriate to their election. An order is a covenant community within the Church to mutually support, care for, and hold accountable its members for the sake of the life and mission of the Church. These orders, separately or together, seek to respond to the spiritual hunger among clergy for a fulfilling sense of vocation, for support among peers during this stressful time of change in the Church, and for a deepening relationship with God.[15]

The distinctive roles and responsibilities of deacons and elders were outlined as follows:

¶319. *The Ministry of a Deacon*—From among the baptized, deacons are called by God to a lifetime of servant leadership, authorized by the Church, and

---

15 UMC *Discipline* 1996, ¶311, p. 179.

ordained by a bishop. Deacons fulfill servant ministry in the world and lead the Church in relating the gathered life of Christians to their ministries in the world, interrelating worship in the gathered community with service to God in the world. Deacons give leadership in the Church's life: in the teaching and proclamation of the Word; in worship, and in assisting the elders in the administration of the sacraments of baptism and the Lord's Supper; in forming and nurturing disciples; in conducting marriages and burying the dead; in the congregation's mission to the world; and in leading the congregation in interpreting the needs, concerns, and hopes of the world. . . .

¶320. *Ministry, Authority, and Responsibilities of Deacons in Full Connection*—1. Deacons are persons called by God, authorized by the Church, and ordained by a bishop to a lifetime ministry of Word and Service to both the community and the congregation in a ministry that connects the two. . . .

¶323. *Ministry of an Elder*—Elders are ordained ministers who, by God's grace, have completed their formal preparation and have been commissioned and served as a probationary member, have been found by the Church to be of sound learning, of Christian character, possessing the necessary gifts and evidence of God's grace, and whose call by God to ordination has been confirmed by the Church. Elders are ordained to a lifetime ministry of Service, Word, Sacrament, and Order. They are authorized to preach and teach the Word of God, to administer the sacraments of baptism and Holy Communion, and to order the life of the Church for mission and ministry. The servant leadership of the elder is expressed by leading the people of God in worship and prayer, by leading persons to faith in Jesus Christ, by exercising pastoral supervision in the congregation, and by leading the Church in obedient mission in the world.[16]

In the latest edition of his *Polity, Practice and the Mission of The United Methodist Church*, Tom Frank summed up the situation this way:

> For the first time in Methodist history, there is an ordained order of persons who do not itinerate and who initiate their own place of employment. Deacons are ordained to "Word and Service," including "proclamation of the Word" (¶¶ 328, 329). But this preaching and service ministry does not participate in the historic understanding of the missionary order of Methodist preachers willing to go where sent. (Local pastors do not have to itinerate, either, but they do not initiate their own employment.) . . . Thus United Methodism is going through fundamental changes in its understanding of set-apart ministry.[17]

The 1996 changes in the order of deacons meant that ordination as a deacon would no longer serve as a necessary step toward ordination as an elder. Consequently, "commissioning" was created in 1996 as a new administrative process and liturgical action to mark the entry of candidates into ministerial service and annual conference membership as probationary elders or deacons:

---

16 UMC *Discipline* 1996, ¶319, pp. 186–87; ¶320, p. 187; ¶323, p. 194.
17 Frank, *Polity, Practice, and the Mission of The United Methodist Church*, 198–99.

¶316. *Commissioning*—Commissioning is the act of the Church that publicly acknowledges God's call according to the talents, gifts and abilities the person has received; the individual's response to that call; the equipping of the person for specialized ministry; the examination by the Church to determine if the gifts meet the needs of the community and world; the validation of that call by the faith community through the laying on of hands; the invocation of the Holy Spirit for empowerment of the person's ministry on behalf of and with the Church community; the commitment of the person to seek avenues of growth to equip others for ministry and to be accountable to the covenant community. The service for commissioning and the service for ordination of deacons and elders may be incorporated into one service symbolizing the total ministry of Jesus Christ. After fulfilling all the candidacy requirements and upon recommendation of the conference board of ordained ministry, the clergy session, composed of elders and deacons in full connection, shall vote on the commissioning of the candidates. The bishop and secretary of the annual conference shall provide credentials to the commissioned minister on commissioning.[18]

At the same time, the function of a local pastor's license was changed to grant probationary elders serving under appointment as pastors the authority for pastoral ministry, including sacramental administration. The basis for this was understood to be ¶341 of the 1996 *Discipline*, which said that "all persons not ordained as elders who are appointed to preach and

---

18 UMC *Discipline* 1996, ¶316, p. 184.

conduct divine worship and perform the duties of a pastor shall have a license as a local pastor." Thus the sacramental authority of probationary elders, like that of local pastors, was understood to flow, not from their ordination (since they were commissioned but not yet ordained), but rather from their licensing and episcopal appointment to pastoral ministry.

John Harnish devotes a full chapter in *The Orders of Ministry in The United Methodist Church* to a discussion of "Commissioning and Ordaining," drawing these distinctions between them: (1) commissioning is temporary, and ordination is for lifetime service; (2) commissioning represents the initial sending of persons into service, while ordination represents identity and authority as an ordained representative of the Church; (3) commissioning marks a step in a journey toward ordination; and (4) ordination is a gift of God, and commissioning is an act of the Church.[19] Harnish is certainly correct in saying that in creating this new liturgical act called *commissioning*, The UMC "has taken the biggest step away from our historic practice and from ecumenical consensus by creating an entirely new office and form of ministry":

> The ecumenical question yet to be answered is how this new, uniquely United Methodist commissioned minister will relate to the orders of other denominations. The notion of non-ordained clergy is an oxymoron in some traditions. Our use of non-ordained local pastors to extend the sacramental ministry of the ordained elder has always raised questions with Roman Catholic, Anglican, and Orthodox traditions, but we have explained this practice as our pragmatic

---

19 Harnish, *The Orders of Ministry in The United Methodist Church*, 82–84; cf. 80–91.

missional exception. Now pastoral leadership including sacramental administration by non-ordained, commissioned clergy will be the standard practice during probation. How we interpret commissioning within the ecumenical community as we seek mutual recognition with other COCU denominations, our sister Methodist denominations, and other Christian churches will be important to our ecumenical relations as well as to our self-understanding. If mutual recognition of orders is to have any integrity, we must meet the demand that we be clear about the forms of ministry we have created and openly acknowledge our uniquely United Methodist ordering of ministry, even if it means straining our ecumenical dialogue.[20]

The paragraph about commissioning was thoroughly rewritten in The UMC *Discipline* 2000:

¶316. *Commissioning*—Commissioning is the act of the church that publicly acknowledges God's call and the response, talents, gifts and training of the candidate. The church invokes the Holy Spirit as the candidate is commissioned to be a faithful servant leader among the people, to lead the church in service, to proclaim the Word of God and to equip others for ministry.

Through commissioning, the church sends persons in leadership and service in the name of Jesus Christ and marks their entrance into a time of probation as they prepare for ordination. Commissioned ministers are probationary clergy members of the annual

---

20 Harnish, *The Orders of Ministry in The United Methodist Church*, 90.

conference and are accountable to the bishop and the clergy session for the conduct of their ministry.

During probation the clergy session discerns their fitness for ordination and their effectiveness in ministry. After fulfilling all candidacy requirements and upon recommendation of the conference board of ordained ministry, the clergy session shall vote on the provisional membership and commissioning of the candidates. The bishop and secretary of the conference shall provide credentials as a probationary member and a commissioned minister in the annual conference.

The period of commissioned ministry is concluded when the probationary members are received as full members of the annual conference and ordained as either deacon or elder, or a decision is made not to proceed toward ordination and probationary membership is ended.[21]

There was no significant textual change in the paragraphs of The UMC *Discipline* 2000 about the authority and responsibilities of deacons (¶¶319–320, pp. 200–201) or elders (¶323, pp. 208–209). The first paragraph concerning the authority and duties of local pastors was modified slightly but significantly:

¶341. *Authority and Duties of License for Pastoral Ministry*—1. Probationary members approved annually by the board of ordained ministry and local pastors approved annually by the district committee on ordained ministry may be licensed by the bishop to perform the duties of a pastor (¶331), including the sacraments of baptism and Holy Communion as well

21 UMC *Discipline* 2000, ¶316, p. 197.

as the service of marriage (where state laws allow), burial, confirmation, and membership reception, while appointed to a particular charge. Local pastors are not eligible for appointment beyond the local church. For the purposes of these paragraphs the charge will be defined as "people within or related to the community being served." While local pastors are not eligible for appointment to extension ministries, probationary members may be appointed to extension ministries approved by the bishop and the board of ordained ministry.[22]

In The UMC *Discipline* 2004, the paragraph about the authority of local pastors was renumbered and revised:

¶316. *Responsibilities and Duties of Those Licensed for Pastoral Ministry*—1. Probationary members approved annually by the board of ordained ministry and local pastors approved annually by the district committee on ordained ministry may be licensed by the bishop to perform the duties of a pastor (¶340), including the sacraments of baptism and Holy Communion as well as the service of marriage (where state laws allow), burial, confirmation, and membership reception, while appointed to a particular charge. For the purposes of these paragraphs the charge will be defined as "people within or related to the community being served." Those licensed for pastoral ministry may be appointed to extension ministry settings when approved by the bishop and the board of ordained ministry.[23]

---

22 UMC *Discipline* 2000, ¶341.1, p. 232.
23 UMC *Discipline* 2004, ¶316, pp. 206–207.

The paragraphs about commissioning (¶325, p. 218) and the authority and responsibilities of deacons (¶¶328–29, pp. 221–22) and elders (¶332, pp. 229–30) were renumbered but not significantly changed. The paragraph outlining the "Responsibilities and Duties of a Pastor" was renamed "Responsibilities and Duties of Elders and Licensed Pastors" and was thoroughly revised and reorganized into three sections: (1) Word and ecclesial acts, (2) Sacrament, and (3) Order (¶340, pp. 238–40).

In The UMC *Discipline* 2008, the paragraphs about commissioning (¶325, pp. 227–28) and the "Responsibilities and Duties of Those Licensed for Pastoral Ministry" (¶316, pp. 214–16) were revised to speak of "provisional elders" rather than "probationary members" but otherwise were not significantly changed. The paragraphs about the authority and responsibilities of deacons (¶¶328–29, pp. 230–32) were similarly revised to speak of "provisional deacons," and significantly changed by the addition of this sentence to ¶328:

> For the sake of extending the mission and ministry of the church, a pastor-in-charge or district superintendent may request that the Bishop grant local sacramental authority to the deacon to administer the sacraments in the absence of an elder, within a deacon's primary appointment.[24]

The debate about this matter on the floor of the 2008 General Conference touched on a number of familiar themes:

> *Laurie A. Haller (West Michigan):* The intent of this petition is to offer sacramental privileges to deacons,

---

24 UMC *Discipline* 2008, ¶328, p. 230.

not for mere convenience, but in extraordinary and special circumstances.

Youtha C. Hardman-Cromwell (Virginia): If we can allow local pastors who are not ordained at all to be allowed by the district superintendents and bishops to offer Communion in the places to which they are appointed, with the restrictions that are in this particular petition surely we can trust ordained deacons to do the same thing.

Kenneth H. Carter (Western North Carolina): Sacramental presidency in the church would cause a shift in the true vocation of the deacon and would lead to confusion or blurring of roles in relation to the orders of deacon and elder, and also the category of local pastor.

Lonnie D. Brooks (Alaska Missionary): This action would put us outside the ecumenical consensus on this matter as it is expressed primarily in the document "Baptism, Eucharist and Ministry" of the World Council of Churches. The United Methodist Church is a signatory to that agreement, and it reserved sacramental authority to elders and not to deacons.

Robin C. Wilson (Alabama-West Florida): There still seems to be much confusion as to what the ministry of the deacon versus the ministry of the elder is; and I worry that if we blur those lines of sacramental authority, that this will be seen by many of our ministerial candidates as a way to circumvent the itinerant system.

Stephan P. Taylor (South Carolina): There are people who need the sacraments in places where deacons are working, and our tradition has always been to let the function go where the people are. Wesley ordained [*unintelligible*] so that the sacraments would go to the people; and we keep sending our people to where the people need them, our ministers, that's why we have local pastors with sacramental authority to be there with the people in certain places that deacons are the ones ministering to the people and the people need the sacraments.

Amy Gearhart Sage (Missouri): This conversation and petition is not about rights. It's not about convenience. It's not about changing the orders. It's about making the means of grace available to all and further extending the ministry and mission of the church. I was compelled most, most profoundly, by a lay person in our Legislative Committee who said, "Please, please don't ever let the Church and its structure deny us the means of grace." That's why we believe as a Legislative Committee that this needs to be adopted, that we might offer the means of grace to others.[25]

The legislation adding the sentence in question to ¶328 was approved by a vote 568 in favor, 282 opposed. The UMC Council of Bishops subsequently adopted guidelines for granting deacons the authority to perform baptisms and to administer Holy Communion under this new and unprecedented provision. The bishops took the position that this "did not fundamentally change the sacramental privileges of the order of deacons." According to the bishops, "local sacramental authority" was to be understood as referring to the primary field of service of the deacon, meaning the immediate community of faith for a congregational appointment or the primary

---

25 UMC/DCA 2008, pp. 2017–2020.

service setting and community for deacons serving beyond a local church.[26]

The paragraph about the authority and responsibilities of elders in The UMC *Discipline* 2008 was revised to read, "By the authority given in their ordination, they are authorized to preach and teach," but otherwise the paragraph was not significantly changed.[27] The beginning sections of the paragraph outlining the "Responsibilities and Duties of Elders and Licensed Pastors" were revised, but the remainder of the paragraph was not significantly changed:

¶340. *Responsibilities and Duties of Elders and Licensed Pastors*—1. The responsibilities of elders are derived from the authority given in ordination. Elders have a fourfold ministry of Word, Sacrament, Order, and Service and thus serve in the local church and in extension ministries in witness and service of Christ's love and justice. Elders are authorized to preach and teach the Word, to provide pastoral care and counsel, to administer the sacraments, and to order the life of the church for service in ministry and mission as pastors, superintendents, and bishops.

2. Licensed pastors share with elders the responsibilities and duties of a pastor for this fourfold ministry, within the context of their appointments.[28]

---

26 Linda Green, "Bishops adopt guidelines on deacons" (undated), UMNS article now posted on the General Board of Higher Education and Ministry website; http://www. gbhem.org/article/bishops-adopt -guidelines-deacons.

27 UMC *Discipline* 2008, ¶332, p. 240.

28 UMC *Discipline* 2008, ¶340, pp. 250–52.

The paragraph on "Responsibilities and Duties of Those Licensed for Pastoral Ministry" (¶316, p. 230) was not significantly changed in The UMC *Discipline* 2012. The paragraph on commissioning (¶325, p. 242) was slightly changed to reflect the introduction of the language of "residency" for those persons commissioned as provisional deacons or elders (see also ¶326). The paragraph on "The Ministry of a Deacon" (¶328, p. 246) was unchanged, but the paragraph on "Ministry, Authority, and Responsibilities of Deacons in Full Connection" was slightly but significantly revised to say that "Deacons are persons called by God, authorized by the Church, and ordained by a bishop to a lifetime ministry of Word, Service, Compassion, and Justice, to both the community and the congregation in a ministry that connects the two."[29] The paragraphs on "Ministry of an Elder," "Elder in Full Connection," and "Responsibilities and Duties of Elders and Licensed Pastors" (¶332–34, pp. 256–59) were not significantly changed.

The 2012 General Conference received a lengthy report produced by the Ministry Study Commission appointed by the 2008 General Conference. One of the key recommendations made by the report was that the practice of commissioning provisional elders and deacons (created in 1996) be eliminated, and that certified candidates be ordained upon the satisfactory completion of all educational and other requirements. "Ordination would mark the entrance into provisional membership and a time of formation and testing in preparation for election to full membership. This change will end the practice of authorizing commissioned leaders to preside at the sacraments." The primary rationale for this was stated by the commission in the section of its report titled "Sacramental Authority":

---

29 UMC *Discipline* 2012, ¶329, pp. 246–47.

Principle: The sacraments are gifts to the church; symbols representing the presence of God in Christ for the transformation of the world through the grace of God. Since the beginning of The United Methodist Church, sacramental authority has been lodged in the Order of Elders. This is consistent with other denominations and signifies both the presidency of Christ at the sacrament and the connection between the local congregation, the denomination, and the ecumenical community. Sacramental authority is rooted in the whole body of Christ, and in United Methodism is passed on through the episcopal office in ordination.

In the case of extraordinary missional need, and where collaborative ministry among elders, deacons, and local pastors is restricted, the bishop may grant sacramental authority to local pastors and deacons. See ¶ 316.1 and ¶ 328 in the *2008 Book of Discipline* for explanation of "missional need" for local pastors and deacons respectively. We are seeking to order the sacramental life of the church in ways that are faithful, missional, clear, flexible, and collegial. We should keep before us the need of the world for the presence of God, particularly the new life symbolized by baptism and the sustaining provision of grace offered in Communion.

Challenge: United Methodism's practical theology has altered the understanding that sacramental presidency resides with the elder for the sake of mission and ministry in some local contexts. As a result The UMC has empowered local pastors and commissioned elders to preside over the sacraments of Holy Communion and baptism in the location where they are appointed. This is a break with ecumenical practices that reserve sacramental authority for the ordained.

Recommendation: Eliminating the practice of commissioning will mean that provisional elders will be ordained as they preside over the sacraments. In addition, annual conferences, under the guidance of resident bishops, should be authorized to make allowance for sacramental practices based on needs within their geographic areas. The commission reiterates that local pastors' presidential authorization is derived through the Order of Elders. Appointment as a local pastor should not automatically include sacramental authority. We expect local pastors to complete the Course of Study and encourage them to continue to move toward satisfying the requirements for ordination as an elder. No disciplinary revisions are recommended.[30]

Very few of the legislative proposals presented to the 2012 General Conference in support of the recommendations of the Ministry Study Commission were approved, and the most significant and far-reaching proposal that was approved, eliminating what is popularly described as the "guaranteed appointment" of elders in full connection, was subsequently ruled unconstitutional by the Judicial Council (see Decision 1226). As a consequence, the actions of the 2012 General Conference, in the end, effected no significant change in the way The UMC understood the relation between commissioning and ordination or the nature of the sacramental authority

---

30 "Summary Report of the Commission for the Study of Ministry 2009–2012," UMC/DCA 2012 Advance Edition, pp. 1381–82; text of full report, pp. 1383–1411; quotation from p. 1391; http://www.umc.org /who-we-are/general-conference-2012-daily-christian-advocate.

of its ministers. Commissioning remained in place as the rite and process through which certified candidates entered their periods of "residency" and service as provisional deacons or elders, a process that normally led to their ordination and election to full annual conference membership.

However, the 2012 General Conference did take a significant action related to ministerial orders and sacramental authority when it approved the ordination of "local elders in mission." The legislative proposal to do this came from the Standing Committee on Central Conference Matters (see UMC/ DCA 2012, p. 2167). The result was the introduction of the following language into The UMC *Discipline* 2012:

¶591.6. The annual meeting of the mission shall have the power to certify candidates for the ordained ministry, to pass on the character of clergy who are not members of an annual conference, to receive mission pastors and local elders in mission, and to recommend to an annual conference proper persons for provisional membership and ordination. The examination of mission pastors and candidates for the local elder in mission shall be held by the mission and certified to an annual conference. *The mission shall have the power to recommend to the correspondent annual conference proper persons for provisional or full membership and ordination as deacons or elders.*

a) Mission pastors are members of the mission without being members of an annual conference. *The mission shall determine the requirements for a mission pastor in order to most effectively utilize the indigenous leadership.* Mission pastors are limited in their itineration to the bounds of the mission.

b) Local elders in mission are ordained members of the mission and are not members of an annual conference. The mission shall, in consultation with the bishop assigned to the mission and the General Board of Global Ministries, recommend the requirements for a local elder in mission. Such recommendations for requirements shall be approved by the Division of Ordained Ministry of the General Board of Higher Education and Ministry. *Local elders in mission are limited in their itineration and sacramental authority to the bounds of the mission and as such are not eligible to transfer their credentials to another annual conference.*[31]

This action took a small step in the direction suggested by Ted A. Campbell in his 2004 article titled "The Oral Roberts Option: The Case for Ordained Local Elders (and Local Deacons?) in The United Methodist Church." Campbell noted that the *Journals* of the Oklahoma Annual Conference of The UMC from 1968 through 1987 carried the name of "Granville Oral Roberts." Dr. Roberts, whose appointment was given as "President, Oral Roberts University, Tulsa," was listed in the *Journals* along with some others in the special category of "Local Elders (before 1968)," that is, those who had been ordained as local elders prior to 1968 and whose status was continued even after the term was disused. Campbell commented on this phenomenon as follows:

It is important to note that the office of local elder, an ordained minister authorized to celebrate the sacrament of Holy Communion, appears in Methodist *Disciplines* through the 1950s, and although the term was disused

---

31 UMC *Discipline* 2012, ¶591, pp. 393–94, italics added.

at a certain point, the provision for local preachers (this was also a distinct office) becoming ordained and thus effectively "local elders" remained in the *Discipline* of the Methodist Church through the last *Discipline* of 1964. The same office (and title, "local elder") appears in the last *Discipline* (1967) of the Evangelical United Brethren Church. It remains in effect in all of our partner churches in the Commission on Pan-Methodist Union and Cooperation, namely the Christian Methodist Episcopal Church, the African Methodist Episcopal Church, and the African Methodist Episcopal Zion Church. The office of local elder remains in effect in many of our international affiliated autonomous churches, such as the *Iglesia Metodista de Mexico* (where local elders are *presbiteros locales*). I believe I am correct in stating that of all these partner churches in the Methodist and Wesleyan tradition, *only The United Methodist Church has taken the unprecedented step of discontinuing the office of local elder and then proceeding to authorize non-ordained persons to celebrate the sacrament of Holy Communion.* We are clearly at odds with our own long tradition in doing so.[32]

Campbell went on to suggest that renewing the office of the local elder might help the church "resolve the difficulties involved in our current practice of authorizing nonordained persons to preside at the Eucharist" and that it could also "bring consistency to our definition of the elder as authorized

---

32 Ted A. Campbell, "The Oral Roberts Option: The Case for Ordained Local Elders (and Local Deacons?) in The United Methodist Church," *Quarterly Review* 24, no. 4 (Winter 2004): 358–66, quotation from 359–60; italics in original.

to preside at Holy Communion (in addition to his or her ministries of preaching the Word and ordering the church)."[33]

The twelve members of the first group to serve in the newly created (or renewed?) ministerial capacity of "local elders in mission" were ordained in January 2013 for the Vietnam Mission Initiative, one of several such missions in Southeast Asia under the direction of the General Board of Global Ministries. George Howard, deputy general secretary of Global Ministries, was quoted as saying that "having ordained elders in mission is a critical building block in developing (the church)." The ordination was performed by Bishop Bruce Ough, now of the Minnesota-Dakotas Episcopal Area. Ough led the West Ohio Episcopal Area when the candidates began their course of studies at United Theological Seminary in Dayton, Ohio. The West Ohio Annual Conference Board of Ordained Ministry supervised and mentored their journey toward ordination, and a delegation from the board traveled to Southeast Asia to interview the candidates prior to their ordination.[34]

The precise, technical definition of *mission* is key to understanding what it means to be ordained as a "local elder in mission." The UMC defines a *mission* as "an administrative body for a field of work inside or outside the structures of any annual conference, provisional annual conference, or missionary conference that is under the care of the General Board of Global Ministries and exercises in a general way the function of a district conference." The purpose of a mission is "to provide ministry with a particular group or region whose needs cannot

---

33 Campbell, "The Oral Roberts Option," 365.
34 Sandra Brands, "Twelve Local Leaders Ordained Local Elders in Mission in Vietnam," GBGM News Report (February 14, 2013); http://www.umc mission.org/Learn-About-Us/News-and-Stories/2013/February/02-14-Twelve-Local Leaders.

be fully met with the existing structures and resources of the annual conference(s)." A mission may also be "the initial stage in moving toward the formation of a provisional or missionary conference."[35]

"Local elders in mission" are, then, somewhat like local pastors, in that they are appointed to service in a particular mission initiative, as local pastors are appointed to a particular church or charge. However, "local elders in mission" are in some ways more like elders, in that they are ordained to word, sacrament, order and service anywhere within the mission initiative through which they itinerate. Further, "local elders in mission" differ from both local pastors and elders in that they are not subject to the educational and other preparation guidelines for commissioning or ordination specified in the *Discipline*; they simply must meet whatever requirements are specified by the mission and its correspondent annual conference. And unlike local pastors, "local elders in mission" clearly derive their authority for sacramental administration, not from their licensing and episcopal appointment, but from the nature of their ordination. However, that sacramental authority is confined within the mission that they serve, and they are not eligible to transfer their credentials to another annual conference.

The 2012 General Conference authorized the creation of a new Commission for the Study of Ministry to work during the 2013–2016 quadrennium. This commission was charged by General Conference with the following tasks:

> The scope of the work will be to provide future research and recommendations on any ministry issue lacking clarity from the 2012 General Conference. Secondly, the work of the Focus Team will be constructive and

---

35 UMC *Discipline* 2012, ¶590, p. 392.

futuristic, examining the following issues that continue to need work:

1. The nature and grounding of the elder;

2. The nature and grounding of the variety of lay ministries;

3. Course of Study and education for local pastors;

4. The status of associate membership;

5. The education of clergy in terms of seminary reform, relevant curriculum, global theological education, funding, and debt of seminary graduates; and

6. The present accountability structure of United Methodist theological schools including the University Senate and Commission on Theological Education.[36]

The 2013–2016 Commission for the Study of Ministry produced a sixty-six-page document, combining its final report and recommend legislative changes for the 2016 General Conference. Among the key recommendations made by the Commission were the following related to "Leadership and the Nature of Ordination":

1. Deepening the theology of ordination: We have proposed legislation clarifying our ordination theology, especially in the introductory paragraphs of each section (see ADCA, ¶¶ 301.1, 301.2, 302, 305, and New Section VI Introduction).

2. Clarifying the relationship between ordination and the sacraments (see ADCA, ¶¶ 316, 328, 340).

---

36 "Summary Report of the 2013–2016 Commission for the Study of Ministry," UMC/DCA 2016 Advance Edition, pp. 1059–61; full report pp. 1062–71; quotation from p. 1059; http://s3.amazonaws.com /Website_Properties/general-conference/2016/documents/gc2016 -advance-daily-christian-advocate-full-english.pdf.

a. All ministry, including the ministry of the laity, deacons, elders, and local pastors, is grounded in the sacraments of baptism and Holy Communion, with baptism as the fundamental initiation into the body of Christ, and called into a life of discipleship.

b. While ministry is born out of baptism, it is sustained in the Eucharistic meal initiated by Jesus Christ's breaking bread with his disciples and giving his own ministry and life for the healing of the world.

c. Administration of the sacraments is an act of receiving God's Spirit to preside at the celebration of God's sacraments.

3. Reshaping the ordination process: We propose that the 2016 General Conference reshape the entry process into ordained ministry, such that persons may be ordained and elected to provisional membership after completing all educational requirements, followed by a residency period, then eligibility for election into full membership (see ADCA, New Section VI).

4. Increasing flexibility for deacons to preside at the celebration of the sacraments (see ADCA, ¶328).[37]

The legislative proposals of the Commission, for revision of ¶¶301 and 302 relating to "Deepening the Theology of Ministry," were assigned to the Faith and Order Legislative Committee. Both were adopted by that committee and approved by the General Conference (see UMC/DCA 2016, calendar items 60481 and 60482).

---

37 UMC/DCA 2016, pp. 1059–60; full report with proposed legislation also available on the website of the General Board of Higher Education and Ministry; https://www.gbhem.org/sites/default/files/documents/publications/StudyofMinistry_Report_And_Legislation.pdf.

The legislative proposal of the Commission for revision of ¶305, relating to "Deepening the Theology of Ordination," was assigned to the Ministry and Higher Education/Superintendency Legislative Committee. The proposal was adopted by that committee and approved by the General Conference (see UMC/DCA 2016, petition 60484.) The revised language of this paragraph more clearly articulates the nature of the ministries of deacons and elders: "Those called to the ministry of deacon are called to witness to the Word in their words and actions, and to embody and lead the community's service in the world for the sake of enacting God's compassion and justice. . . . Those called to the ministry of elder are called to bear authority and responsibility to preach and teach the Word, to administer the sacraments, and to order the life of the church so it can be faithful in making disciples of Jesus Christ for the transformation of the world."[38]

The legislative proposals of the Commission related to ¶¶316 and 340, concerning "Clarifying the Relation between Ordination and the Sacraments," along with the proposed new introduction to Section VI, "Provisional Membership" (¶¶324–336), were assigned to the Ministry and Higher Education/Superintendency Legislative Committee. These proposals were not adopted by that committee and so were never considered by the full General Conference.[39]

The legislative proposal of the Commission related to ¶328, "The Ministry of a Deacon," was adopted by the Ministry and Higher Education/Superintendency Legislative Committee, presented to the full General Conference, and approved after amendment on the floor. This legislation had the effect of removing the old "in the absence of an elder" language

---

38 UMC *Discipline* 2016, ¶305, p. 227.
39 See UMC "2016 Legislative Tracking"; http://calms2016.umc.org.

restricting the circumstances in which a deacon could be authorized by her or his bishop to celebrate the sacraments. The relevant part of the revised paragraph reads as follows: "For the sake of extending the mission and ministry of the church and offering the means of grace to the world, the resident bishop of the annual conference in which the deacon is appointed may authorize the deacon to preside at the celebration of the sacraments."[40]

On balance, it must be said that the proposals and recommendations of the 2013–2016 Commission for the Study of Ministry were not fully embraced by 2016 General Conference. Some significant changes were enacted, particularly relating to the sacramental authority of deacons, but the General Conference was not willing to accept the proposals of the commission to significantly reshape The UMC's ordination process by abandoning the process of "commissioning," separating ordination from annual conference membership, and adopting the practice of ordaining candidates for deacon or elder at the completion of their educational requirements.

The 2016 General Conference did approve the establishment of a new Commission for the Study of Ministry for the 2017–2020 quadrennium (see UMC/DCA p. 2464, Petition 60509, 18 May 2016). The mandate of this new commission is as follows:

1. Articulate a theology of ordained ministry for The United Methodist Church in consultation with the Committee on Faith and Order;

2. Explore and clarify the relationship between the ministry structures in the 2016 *Book of Discipline* and a possible *General Book of Discipline*. The Commission for the Study of Ministry should provide guidance and

---

40 UMC *Discipline* 2016, ¶328, p. 253.

language in the development of text for the *General Book of Discipline*, Chapter Two—"The Ministry of the Ordained"—and Chapter Three—"The Superintendency." Members of the Commission for the Study of the Ministry shall be on the writing committee for the *General Book of Discipline*;

3. Further examine the formation and education of clergy, working toward a systemic model that embraces both Master of Divinity and Course of Study work, and continues into provisional membership and the early years of ministry. The commission should also reflect on the possibility of allowing annual conference Boards of Ordained Ministry to consider persons for ordination who have completed advanced degrees (beyond the bachelor's degree) in fields relevant to ministry when those degrees are integrated with basic graduate theological studies at an approved seminary;

4. Examine funding sources and patterns for theological and ministry education and formation;

5. Explore student debt accumulated by United Methodist seminary graduates and ways to reduce costs.[41]

---

41 See UMC "2016 Legislative Tracking," Petition 60509; http://calms 2016.umc.org.

Observations and Reflections

(1) Perceived "pastoral necessity" (or missional urgency) has generally trumped sacramental theology throughout the history of American Methodism.

It was the fact that people needed access to the sacraments and there were no priests in the wilderness of the Delmarva Peninsula that prompted the early American preacher Robert Strawbridge to begin his maverick sacramental ministry. He continued his sacramental practices until his death in 1781, ignoring the clear prohibition on administration of the sacraments by unordained preachers enacted by the first American Methodist Conference in 1773.

It was "pastoral necessity" that led a group of Methodist preachers meeting in 1779 in Fluvanna, Virginia, to form a presbytery and ordain each other so that they could provide the sacraments to their people. Francis Asbury succeeded in persuading them to place a moratorium on their sacramental administration while an appeal for guidance and direction was made to John Wesley. It was "pastoral necessity" that led Wesley to take the step of ordination, in order to provide for access to the sacraments by the Methodist people in America, and this, in turn, led to the formation of the Methodist Episcopal

Church in 1784. It is worth noting that neither the preachers at Fluvanna nor John Wesley himself could conceive of a solution to the sacramental crisis engendered by the American Revolution that did *not* involve ordination. For Mr. Wesley and the earliest generations of Methodists, a pastor's sacramental authority was inextricably related to and necessarily derived from ordination as an elder, not from election to membership in an Annual Conference or from episcopal appointment to a particular church or charge.

Since 1784, the "pastoral necessity" of providing access to the sacraments for people otherwise deprived of them has led repeatedly to decisions by Methodist church bodies to grant to deacons (despite the nature of their ordination) and/or unordained preachers (despite their lack of ordination) the authority to baptize and to administer Holy Communion:

- The MPC decision to allow unordained pastors to baptize, to perform marriage ceremonies, and to administer the Lord's Supper (1900);
- The MECS decisions to allow unordained pastors to baptize and to perform marriage ceremonies (1906), and to administer the Lord's Supper (1926);
- The MEC decision to allow unordained pastors to baptize and perform marriages, but not administer the Lord's Supper (1912);
- The MC decision to follow the MPC and the MECS, not the MEC, by allowing unordained pastors to baptize, to perform marriage ceremonies, and to administer the Lord's Supper (1939);
- The MC decision to allow both deacons and unordained preachers serving as local pastors to administer Lord's Supper under certain conditions (1952);

- The UMC decisions to continue the MC pattern, allowing deacons (1968) and unordained local pastors (1976) to baptize, to perform marriage ceremonies, and to administer the Lord's Supper "when serving as a regularly appointed pastor in charge" of a church or charge;
- The UMC decision to extend sacramental authority to members of the post-1996 order of deacons within their "primary appointment" under certain conditions and with episcopal approval (2008);
- The UMC decision "increasing flexibility for deacons to preside at the celebration of the sacraments" by allowing resident bishops to authorize deacons to celebrate the sacraments without restriction to their "primary appointment" (2016);

Time after time throughout the history of American Methodism, "pastoral necessity" (or missional urgency) has been a driving force, and the principles of *expediency* and *utility* have been primary factors in such decisions.[1]

(2) The practical theology of American Methodism has said in effect that sacramental authority flows from episcopal appointment (or annual conference authorization) as well as, or instead of, from ordination.

This practical theology is apparent in the decisions of The UMC and all of its antecedents to allow unordained preachers serving as local pastors to have authority to administer the sacraments, by virtue of their appointment to their charge by their bishop (or in the MPC, with the approval of their Annual Conference)—the only exception being that the MEC did not

---

1   See Bangs, *A History of the Methodist Episcopal Church*, 2:314–16.

allow unordained pastors to serve the Lord's Supper. It is perhaps most obvious in the 2008 UMC decision to allow deacons to have "local sacramental authority" in certain special circumstances as a consequence of episcopal action. Since 1996, deacons in The UMC have been ordained to "a lifetime ministry of Word and Service" (since 2012, of "Word, Service, Compassion, and Justice)," whereas elders are ordained to "a lifetime ministry of Service, Word, Sacrament, and Order" (since 2008, of "Word, Sacrament, Order, and Service"). Nevertheless, The UMC allows bishops to grant sacramental authority to deacons, in certain situations, within their "primary appointment," which means that despite the nature of their ordination as deacons they can be authorized by their bishop to baptize and to serve Holy Communion.

Since the sacramental authority (however restricted) of deacons in The UMC cannot flow from their ordination, it must flow from episcopal appointment. The same is true of local pastors, who by definition are not ordained and yet have sacramental authority in the charges to which they are appointed, by virtue of their licensing and episcopal appointment. The consequence of all this has been a disconnection between ordination and sacramental authority, resulting in significant confusion, especially among lay people in local congregations but also among some members of the clergy, about the nature, purpose, and effects of ordination, and also about the differences among elders, deacons, and local pastors serving under appointment as pastors-in-charge.

(3) American Methodism has a long-standing tension between a "sacramental" view and a "functional" view of ordination.

A "sacramental" view of ordination holds that sacramental authority is conveyed to a person by God through the ordination rite, when the hands of a bishop are laid upon the candidate as the work of the Holy Spirit is invoked. A "functional" view of ordination stresses the authorization by a congregation or community of an individual to assume ministerial office and to celebrate the sacraments on behalf of that community. Randy Maddox has helpfully characterized the difference between these contrasting views of the nature of ordination as follows:

> In the strictest "sacramental" model, ordination is expressed in its full sense in the ordination of a bishop (by other bishops!), which confers the grace to sanctify others; bishops ordain priests, conferring to them the grace to sanctify the sacraments (as an extension of the ministry of the bishop). The emphasis is on ordination "infusing" the gift of the Spirit; and it is considered to be enduring (for life, unless specifically annulled; and unrepeatable). . . .
>
> In the purest "functional" model, the community recognizes those whom the Holy Spirit has given individually the proper gifts, and "authorizes" them to serve a specific function in the church; the ordination is an act of the community, and is revocable by the community.[2]

The tension between these views of the nature of ordination can be clearly seen throughout the history of American Methodism and is expressed at numerous points in the General Conference debates recounted above. That tension is also evident in the differing positions of recent scholarly works on

---

2 Randy L. Maddox, "Ordained Ministry in The United Methodist Church: Some Historical/Theological Perspectives on Present Concerns," presentation to the 2013–2016 UMC Ministry Study Commission at its meeting in Durham, NC, 28–30 October 2013 (unpublished, used with permission).

ministry in the United Methodist tradition. For example, Dennis M. Campbell has articulated a strongly "sacramental" view of the nature of ordination:

> The church confirms the call of God in candidates for the ministry and decides who should be its ordained leaders, but in the act of ordination itself, the principal actor is God, through the Holy Spirit. The gathered assembly invokes God's presence, and prays that the grace of the Holy Spirit will be given to empower the ministry of the one ordained for the sake of the church. The emphasis is on what God is doing for the church, through the provision of leadership for sacramental ministries, preaching and proclamation, teaching, prophetic ministries, and the ordering and governance of the community. . . . The ordained minister is not an individual actor, but one who is serving in an office commissioned by the church for its good. It is an office given by God, and accepted and continued by the church. . . .
>
> What, exactly does ordination do to the one ordained? . . . Sometimes popular Protestant thinking has reduced ordination to a kind of credentialing. Most Protestant theology, however, has emphasized the reality of ordination as God's act, through the Holy Spirit, in the church. In this sense, ordination does alter the identity of the one who is ordained, because that person is bound to the fullness of the church and its ministry, and becomes an official representative person of and to the church. . . . Ordination is a gift of

God to help assure apostolicity, catholicity, and unity, signs of the church of Jesus Christ.[3]

By contrast, John Harnish is of the opinion that

It is fair to say that, historically, Methodism's understanding of ordination has been primarily functional, even when some of those functions were also granted to non-ordained persons. The ordained were set apart for special functions (including sacraments, preaching, and ordering or superintending) in service to the whole church and for the sake of the ministry of the whole people of God.[4]

More recently, Bill Lawrence has emphatically echoed Harnish's views and advanced a strongly "functional" view of the nature and effects of ordination:

The ordained ministry in Methodism is a set of offices which are occupied by persons who have been designated by the church to fulfill these offices for the sake of the church. . . . Those who are ordained . . . have been given a mandate by the church, and will be held accountable by the church. . . .

Ordination must always be understood as entry into an office that one occupies, not as an identity that one has been granted or that one owns. An individual who is ordained does not undergo a transformation of human character. . . . Every ordinand will remain blessed with the same gifts, burdened with the same limitations, driven by the same hopes, and drained by

---

3 Campbell, *Who Will Go for Us? An Invitation to Ordained Ministry,* 76–79.

4 Harnish, *The Orders of Ministry in The United Methodist Church,* 68.

the same frailties that dwelt in their souls before the service began.

Moreover, within Methodism, ordained ministry is not something that belongs to the individual. To be ordained is not to acquire a status that one lacked prior to ordination. To be ordained is to enter into an office that belongs to the church. It is a kind of tenancy. One occupies the office as long as the church deems it appropriate to be the case. . . . One never owns one's ordination.[5]

Laceye Warner seems to have a similarly "functional" view of ordination in her recently published textbook on UM polity, when she says that "in ordination individuals are set apart for ministry, though . . . an individual may be called to pastoral ministry but not called to ordination."[6] In contrast, Tom Frank has expressed a view that is a kind of *via media* between the "sacramental" and "functional" understandings of the nature of ordination, and suggests that the "hesitancy" of United Methodism between these views may be due to its "ambiguous understanding of the place of Holy Communion":

Only elders are specifically ordained to administration of this sacrament, echoing the priestly understanding from Anglicanism and Catholicism. Yet United Methodism also permits a host of nonordained persons—local pastors under appointment—to administer communion in their charges. This leads to a more presidential or pastoral understanding, that the pastor presides for

---

5   Lawrence, *Ordained Ministry in The United Methodist Church*, 17–18.

6   Warner, *The Method of Our Mission*, 73, cf. 73–76.

the good order of the community of faith and thus is acting on behalf of the whole people of God.

The flexibility of all this terminology mirrors United Methodism's middling ecclesiological view of ministry. The ordained are set apart for specialized ministry, but remain part of the people of God. They must be ordained by a bishop, but not for the sake of apostolic succession, only for the sake of good order. . . . In common with all the people of God, "specialized" ministers have a calling by the power of the Holy Spirit. That call must be confirmed by the community of faith.[7]

(4) The practice of allowing unordained local pastors (and under certain circumstances, deacons) to have sacramental authority by virtue of their licensing and/or episcopal appointment puts The UMC in a tenuous situation both theologically and ecumenically.

In particular, this UMC practice appears to contradict some of the foundational theological principles articulated on the basis of ecumenical consensus in the *Baptism, Eucharist and Ministry* (*BEM*) document of the World Council of Churches, of which The UMC is a member. This contradiction was noted in a United Methodist News Service article published in advance of the 2012 General Conference, which seems in retrospect to have been prescient:

In response to the World Council of Churches document *Baptism, Eucharist and Ministry*, which outlined the broadest ecumenical theological convergence in modern church history, The United Methodist Church conducted studies on baptism and on the Eucharist.

---

7 Frank, *Polity, Practice, and the Mission of The United Methodist Church*, 166–67.

Those studies produced two documents—*By Water and the Spirit* and *This Holy Mystery*—that now guide our church both theologically and practically in its understanding and practice of the sacraments.

The first United Methodist Church Ministry Study Commission drew excitement across the church as many of us hoped for the same process that guided our studies of baptism and Eucharist. The theological convergence that grounds our sacramental life in the best biblical, theological and historical wisdom is also available to guide our understandings of ministry and ordination.

Yet, for two quadrennia, we have walked away from the ministry section of *Baptism, Eucharist and Ministry* and produced a report that offers little theological clarity on the meaning of ordination, orders and the practice of ministry. Without a coherent understanding of ordination, the proposal coming to the 2012 General Conference wants us to ordain people at the entrance to a provisional process where, if they fail to meet the requirements for full conference membership, they face the prospect of something like being "unordained."

The study commission states that it was operating under a mandate from the 2008 General Conference to separate conference membership and ordination, and the result is a proposal in which conference membership obviously trumps ordination. Not only have we separated them; we also have demonstrated that our preference for practical solutions to ministry issues operates without any guiding understanding of ordination.

Another puzzling proposal on sacramental authority attempts to solve the ecumenical embarrassment we face in authorizing non-ordained persons to celebrate the Eucharist by clarifying that it resides in the office of ordained elder. In the same breath, it grants bishops the authority to give that Eucharistic presidency to non-ordained licensed persons as well as ordained deacons in certain missional settings.

What guides our understanding of ordination, not to mention Eucharistic presidency? It is obvious we have no coherent theology of ordination and continue to justify various proposed actions out of supposed missional urgency.[8]

Contrast this characterization of the position of The UMC with the discussion of the eucharistic celebration in *BEM*:

It is especially in the eucharistic celebration that the ordained ministry is the visible focus of the deep and all-embracing communion between Christ and the members of his body. In the celebration of the eucharist, Christ gathers, teaches and nourishes the Church. It is Christ who invites to the meal and who presides at it. In most churches this presidency is signified and represented by an ordained minister.[9]

And compare the current structures and practices of ministerial orders in The UMC with the exposition of the classic threefold pattern of ordained ministry in *BEM*:

---

8 Daniel L. Garrett, "Ministry study: a missed opportunity?" United Methodist News Service (April 18, 2012); http://umcconnections .org/2012/04/18/ ministry-study-a-missed-opportunity-2/.

9 See *Baptism, Eucharist and Ministry*, Faith and Order Paper no. 111 (Geneva: World Council of Churches, 1982), 14–15.

Bishops preach the Word, preside at the sacraments, and administer discipline in such a way as to be representative pastoral ministers of oversight, continuity and unity in the Church. They have pastoral oversight of the area to which they are called. They serve the apostolicity and unity of the Church's teaching, worship and sacramental life. They have responsibility for leadership in the Church's mission. They relate the Christian community in their area to the wider Church, and the universal Church to their community. They, in communion with the presbyters and deacons and the whole community, are responsible for the orderly transfer of ministerial authority in the Church.

Presbyters serve as pastoral ministers of Word and sacraments in a local eucharistic community. They are preachers and teachers of the faith, exercise pastoral care, and bear responsibility for the discipline of the congregation to the end that the world may believe and that the entire membership of the Church may be renewed, strengthened and equipped in ministry. Presbyters have particular responsibility for the preparation of members for Christian life and ministry.

Deacons represent to the Church its calling as servant in the world. By struggling in Christ's name with the myriad needs of societies and persons, deacons exemplify the interdependence of worship and service in the Church's life. They exercise responsibility in the worship of the congregation: for example by reading the scriptures, preaching and leading the people in prayer. They help in the teaching of the congregation. They exercise a ministry of love within the community.

They fulfill certain administrative tasks and may be elected to responsibilities for governance.[10]

In *By Water and the Spirit* and *This Holy Mystery*, The UMC has carefully thought through theologically profound and practically useful expositions of baptism and Holy Communion that resonate with the ecumenical consensus of *BEM* yet are distinctive to United Methodism. The UMC badly needs a comparably deep, detailed, and thorough exposition of its theology and practice of ordination, ministerial orders, and sacramental authority.

(5) American Methodism has, since 1784, been characterized by a "dual framework" of authorization for ministry; the 1996 ministry legislation challenged this "dual framework."

Initially, none of the Methodist preachers in America (and very few in England other than John and Charles Wesley) were ordained, and Methodism was understood to be a reforming movement within the Church of England. The Methodist movement and its groups and activities were supplemental to regular worship in local parish churches, where people would have regular access to the sacraments. Methodist preachers were accepted into that role on the basis of an examination of their "gifts, grace and fruits" and continued so long as they remained faithful and effective in their preaching ministry.

After the formation of the MEC in 1784, formal membership in the Methodist conference (after 1796, one of the geographically defined annual conferences) became the basic framework for the authorization of Methodist ministry. All of the traveling preachers were annual conference members;

---

10 *Baptism, Eucharist and Ministry*, 24–25.

some were also ordained as elders or deacons. The sense long persisted, as Tom Frank has observed, that "ordination of elders was a pragmatic setting-apart of persons under definite needs of the traveling ministry in certain situations and contexts":

> As a consequence of the privileging of preaching and the pragmatic root of ordination, United Methodism continues to authorize the ministry of elders in two separate, sometimes parallel, sometimes discordant, frameworks. The one with clear priority, as demonstrated often by the grammar of the *Discipline*, is annual conference relationship. The other is ordination, which derives its importance not so much from its intrinsic value as from its relationship with credentials for full conference membership.[11]

In short, annual conference membership was at first primary; ordination was secondary. But with the passage of time, "the status conferred by ordination became the distinguishing mark of full conference membership." Local pastors have always presented a challenge to this dual framework, since they are understood to be clergy members of their annual conference but are not members in the same sense as elders and deacons in "full connection." And as Frank has observed, the ministry legislation of 1996 brought about a yet more serious challenge to the traditional dual framework of authorization for Methodist ministry:

> The 1996 ministry plan . . . disengages the dual tracks by eliminating ordination for those "on trial" (the historic language) as elders and members in full connection in

---

11 Frank, *Polity, Practice, and the Mission of The United Methodist Church*, 196–97.

an annual conference. Probationary [after 2008, provisional] members are "commissioned" for their work, a minimum of three years in which they are "commissioned ministers," but not ordained as deacons—the historic practice (¶325 [2004 *Discipline*]).

Thus United Methodism is going through fundamental changes in its understanding of set-apart ministry. In true synthetic fashion, The UMC seeks to maintain itineracy and superintendency as its definitive practices, even while moving toward a model that could greatly increase the number of clergy who are hired by local churches and do not itinerate. How this will settle out, only time will tell.[12]

In creating the 2009–2012 Ministry Study Commission, the 2008 General Conference charged it to "report to the 2012 General Conference with legislation addressing the issues before the Commission including the ordering of ministry, the separation of ordination and conference membership, and the streamlining of the process leading toward ordained ministry." In its report to the 2012 General Conference, the Study of Ministry Commission made nine recommendations, including the following:

[The commission] recommends that certified candidates be ordained upon the satisfactory completion of all educational and other requirements, and recommends the elimination of commissioning. Ordination would mark the entrance into provisional membership and a time of formation and testing in preparation for election to full membership. This change will end the

---

12 Frank, *Polity, Practice, and the Mission of The United Methodist Church*, 198–99.

practice of authorizing commissioned leaders to pre-side at the sacraments.[13]

The legislation supporting this recommendation would have amended "all paragraphs of the *Book of Discipline* that deal with or are affected by commissioning of candidates for ordained ministry in order to discontinue that practice and place ordination in the process where commissioning now stands."[14] This would have had the effect of restoring the tra-ditional "dual framework" for the authorization of ministry for both deacons and elders, but it would have done so by making ordination a first step with election to full conference member-ship a second and subsequent step. This raised a serious ques-tion: "What happens to people if they are ordained but then *not* elected to full conference membership? Are they somehow 'un-ordained'?"

The legislation supporting the commission's recommenda-tion was not supported in the General Conference legislative committee by an overwhelming margin of 74–0 (2 not voting). The 2016 General Conference legislative committee rejected similar proposals by a correspondingly large majority (58–23).[15] As a result, the practice of commissioning provisional elders and deacons, rather than ordaining them, remains in place. Ordina-tion continues to follow, not precede, election to full annual conference membership. This reveals a continuing lack of clarity

---

13 "Summary Report of the Commission for the Study of Ministry 2009–2012," UMC/DCA 2012 Advance Edition, p. 1381; http://www.umc.org /who-we-are/general-conference-2012-daily-christian-advocate.

14 "General Conference 2012: Legislation Tracking," Petition 20288-MH-¶325; http://www.umc.org/who-we-are/general-conference-2012 -legislation-tracking.

15 UMC "2016 Legislation Tracking," Petition 60507; http://calms2016 .umc.org.

OBSERVATIONS AND REFLECTIONS

and consensus about exactly what The UMC understands to be the nature, meaning, purpose, and effects of ordination.

(6) The practice of commissioning rather than ordaining provisional deacons and elders continues to be a source of significant misunderstanding and confusion in The UMC.

John Harnish had it exactly right when he said, "The creation of the liturgical act of commissioning may well prove to be one of the most helpful and creative acts of the 1996 ministry legislation, or it may be the most confusing and misunderstood aspect of our new ordering of ministry."[16] Across the past two decades, the latter has proven to be true in far too many cases. The relation and distinction between commissioning and ordination is not well understood in theory, nor is it consistently maintained in practice across The UMC. Despite the best efforts of staff members of the General Board of Discipleship to revise the United Methodist *Ordinal* so as to effectively distinguish the services of commissioning and of ordination, some bishops and annual conferences are very intentional about keeping these services separate and distinct, but others celebrate them together as part of the same liturgical service.[17] Stories abound of local congregations giving the stole of an elder to their newly commissioned pastor, of whom they are so proud, only to be disappointed and confused when she has to tell them that she can't wear it because she isn't really ordained yet. "Wait just a minute—you can marry us

---

16 Harnish, *The Orders of Ministry in The United Methodist Church*, 91.

17 Compare the order of service for the commissioning of provisional members with the orders of service for the ordination of deacons and of elders in the most recent edition of The UMC Ordinal; https://www.umcdiscipleship.org//resources/services-for-ordering-of-ministry-in-the-united-methodist-church-2017-2020.

and bury us and baptize us and serve us Holy Communion, right? So what do you mean when you say that you're not really ordained yet, and so you can't wear that stole?"

The 2004 General Conference created a twenty-five-member Ministry Study Commission to address "the continued ambiguity in the denomination's understanding of lay, licensed, and ordained ministry." That commission brought a report to the 2008 General Conference, saying that it had reached consensus that "the 1996 legislation making commissioning the first step toward ordination is problematic" and that "the process for entry into ordained ministry and full conference membership needs to be more timely, efficient, encouraging and motivating, as well as more relevant to age and life experience." In its study document, the commission proposed "separating ordination from entrance into full connection in the life of the church" and agreed that "a candidate first will be ordained either as deacon or elder, and then must serve two years in residence under the supervision of the cabinet and the board of ordained ministry before being eligible for full conference membership." But because it was unable to reach consensus on all the details of how to implement these principles, the commission recommended an additional four years of study.[18]

The 2008 General Conference approved recommendation for an additional quadrennium of study, and as a result another Ministry Study Commission was established for the 2009–2012 quadrennium. The results of the work of that commission, as noted above, included a recommendation to the 2012 General Conference that commissioning be eliminated and that approved candidates be ordained as deacons or elders at the

---

18 Linda Green, "Commission wants further study of church's ministry," UMNS article (April 17, 2007); http://www.umc.org/news-and-media /commission-wants-further-study-of-church's-ministry.

completion of their educational requirements. The legislation that would have implemented that recommendation was not approved by the 2012 General Conference. The same was the result of the work of the 2013–2016 Commission for the Study of Ministry; the 2016 General Conference again maintained the status quo in regard to commissioning, ordination, and annual conference membership.

(7) Changing demographics and financial constraints are forcing The UMC to be increasingly reliant on unordained local pastors to provide the sacraments to local church communities.

For several years, the Lewis Center for Church Leadership at Wesley Theological Seminary has been gathering and analyzing statistical data on UM clergy. One of the major concerns of the Lewis Center has been clergy age trends, in particular the aging of the cohort of elders in the five jurisdictional conferences of The UMC and the drop during the last twenty years in the number of elders under the age of 35. However, in the summary of its 2014 report, the Lewis Center also notes the declining number of elders in comparison to the growing number of local pastors:

> Elders and local pastors are appointed as pastors of congregations. The number of active elders continues to decline as the number of local pastors grows. Since 1990 there are 6,123 fewer elders and 3,459 more local pastors. In 1990 there were over five elders for each local pastor; today there are two elders for each local pastor. In 2014 there are 15,384 elders and 7,395 local pastors.
>
> Elders between ages 55 and 72 comprise 55 percent of all active elders, the highest percentage in

history. This group reached 50 percent for the first time ever in 2010. This age cohort represented only 30 percent of active elders as recently as 2000. Previously their percentage of the total was even lower.

The median age of elders increased to 56 in 2014, the highest in history. The median age was 50 in 2000 and 45 in 1973. The average age remains at 53, an historic high, though unchanged for five years. The mode age (the single age most represented) remains at 61, also a high.

The percentage of elders aged 35 to 54 continues to shrink, from 65 percent of all active elders in 2000 to 39 percent in 2014.

The number of young elders hit an historic low in 2005 and has increased by almost 100 (or about 12 percent) since then. The number of young local pastors and deacons, while much lower than elders, has increased at a higher rate since 2005. Today those under-35 make up about six percent of elders, nine percent of deacons, and eight percent of local pastors.[19]

The following table was constructed using historical data from the records of the Lewis Center to show the total numbers of elders, deacons, and local pastors in the five jurisdictional conferences of The UMC from 2006 through 2016. As this table indicates, in 2016, local pastors made up 32.1 percent of the total number of persons serving as ministers in The UMC; this is up from 26.3 percent a decade earlier. In contrast, the percentage of elders has declined from 70.4 percent in 2006

---

19 Lewis Center for Church Leadership, "Clergy Age Trends in The United Methodist Church: 2014 Report"; https://www.churchleader ship.com/wp-content/uploads/2016/04/ClergyAgeTrends14.pdf.

Year	Elders	Deacons	Local Pastors	Total
2006	18,005 (70.4%)	844 (3.3%)	6,731 (26.3%)	25,580
2007	17,800 (69.6%)	902 (3.5%)	6,863 (26.8%)	25,565
2008	17,480 (68.9%)	897 (3.5%)	6,981 (27.5%)	25,358
2009	17,254 (68.1%)	915 (3.6%)	7,164 (28.3%)	25,333
2010	17,293 (67.6%)	930 (3.6%)	7,341 (28.7%)	25,564
2011	16,954 (67.1%)	949 (3.8%)	7,353 (29.1%)	25,256
2012	16,601 (66.1%)	972 (3.9%)	7,532 (30.0%)	25,105
2013	16,289 (65.3%)	973 (3.9%)	7,671 (30.8%)	24,933
2014	15,384 (64.8%)	954 (4.0%)	7,395 (31.2%)	23,733
2015	15,019 (64.1%)	954 (4.1%)	7,464 (31.8%)	23,437
2016	14,665 (63.5%)	1,003 (4.4%)	7,408 (32.1%)	23,076

to 63.5 percent in 2016.[20] Since local pastors are by definition unordained men and women who are appointed to serve as pastors in charge of a local church or charge, this table shows that nearly one-third of the churches or charges in the five jurisdictional conferences are currently served by unordained clergy. When one adds to that fact the reality that many local pastors are appointed to charges consisting of two or more local churches, the percentage of churches currently served by unordained clergy rises significantly and may well begin to approach one-half. If one then takes into account the fact that a number of ordained elders serve as staff in large churches with multiple

---

20 Note that the data collected for this project does not include the Central Conferences of The UMC outside the U.S. Comparable data for the Central Conferences is not readily available.

clergy, or receive appointments to various extension ministries (see UMC *Discipline* 2012, ¶344, p. 272; UMC *Discipline* 2016, ¶344, 288–81), the number of elders actually available for appointment as pastors in charge is considerably less than the totals shown in the table at the top of page 125.[21]

In a UMNS story about the Lewis Center's 2014 report, Lovett Weems, director of the center, observed that the number of full-time local pastors had dipped slightly, but that the number of part-time local pastors continued to climb. He added that the explanation for this lay, at least in part, in the increasing number of congregations whose dwindling and aging membership and falling attendance left them with serious financial constraints: "I do think the declining number of churches able to afford a full-time pastor is a key indicator that we need to be attuned to."[22] The data from the 2016 report shows that these trends have accelerated.

(8) If The UMC is increasingly reliant on local pastors to do the pastoral work of elders, should not The UMC provide for their ordination?

In a pair of articles prepared for and presented to the 2009 Ministry Study Symposium held at Garret-Evangelical Theological Seminary, as part of the work of the 2009–2012 UMC Ministry Study Commission, E. Byron Anderson made precisely this proposal in persuasive terms:

> United Methodist discipline, polity, and practice have consistently stated that ministerial order is defined by

---

21 On extension ministers, see Russell E. Richey, *Extension Ministers: Mr. Wesley's True Heirs* (Nashville: General Board of Higher Education and Ministry, UMC, 2008).

22 Sam Hodges, "Church continues to see clergy aging trend," UMNS (Sept. 3, 2014); http://www.nyac.com/newsdetail/417149.

function, and that the functions of Word, Sacrament, Service, and Order define the order of elder. Yet, as the [*Discipline*] makes clear, local pastors are authorized for precisely these functions. In practice and in responsibility, there is little that distinguishes the local pastor from the ordained elder other than the fact/rite of ordination itself. As an "un-ordained elder" is a contradiction in terms, it becomes clear not only that the local pastor and ordained elder are not of different orders, but also that local pastors should be publicly authorized for their ministry by ordination.[23]

Anderson here seems to advocate a "sacramental" rather than a "functional" understanding of the nature of ordination, and supports his views with the following arguments:

First, local pastors "share with the elders the responsibilities and duties of a pastor" and carry a pastoral authority "derived from the authority given in ordination" as elder (*Book of Discipline* [2008], ¶340). Second, the purpose of the local pastor is for pastoral care in one specific location (making the appointment of a local pastor to a variety of charges, as is occurring in some annual conferences, a contradiction in terms and a violation of discipline). Third, since approval of a constitutional amendment in 2005, local pastors have standing as clergy members of an annual conference. (They are not elected to membership, but are granted

---

23 E. Byron Anderson, "Postscript: Elders and Local Pastors," unpublished paper presented at the Garret-Evangelical Theological Seminary Ministry Study Symposium (2009), 2. This is a follow-up to his major presentation to the symposium, "Sacramental Ministry and Ordination in The United Methodist Church." Used by permission.

such standing by virtue of, and for the term of, their appointment to a congregation.) What distinguishes the local pastor from the ordained elder (as well as deacon) in this standing is the local pastor's inability to vote on such things as clergy standing and constitutional decisions.

The first of these points is most important to my argument: If the responsibilities, duties, and authority of the local pastor and elder are the same, and derive from "the authority given in ordination," then it is clear that local pastors do not constitute an order different from the order of elders. Another way of saying this is suggested by Nicholas Taylor, in his historical survey of the relationship between sacramental ministry and ordination: if we "lawfully authorize" a lay person "to exercise the functions and office of a priest, such as preaching or administering the sacraments," they "thereby become a priest, even if not episcopally ordained" [Nicholas Taylor, *Lay Presidency at the Eucharist? An Anglican Approach* (New York and London: Mowbray, 2009), 107]. While "lawfully authorized but not ordained," local pastors engage in the same ministry at the level of the local church as do elders. Given the shared responsibilities and similar standing in the annual conference, what we have done with local pastors can be more accurately described as creating a category of "temporary elders" for whom we have waived the educational and covenantal requirements of "permanent elders." Rather than create a separate order of local pastors, a more consistent response would be to argue that if we appoint a person as pastor (or pastor-in-charge) of a congregation with all of the responsibilities and duties of that office, that person should be ordained, as ordination conveys the authority for that office.[24]

Perhaps building on the 2012 decision to create the office of "local elder in mission" offers a way forward here. Ted Campbell (among others) has suggested the renewal of the office of local elder, once so important in the MEC and the MECS, as a way to deal with the issue of the sacramental authority of local pastors in The UMC today.[25] Perhaps the office of local pastor could be combined with that of local elder in mission. If The UMC considers it essential that those who serve as local elders in mission have full sacramental authority in their appointed areas of pastoral service by virtue of ordination, it seems difficult to understand why those who serve as local pastors should not also have sacramental authority in the churches or charges to which they are appointed by virtue of ordination, rather than simply by license and episcopal appointment.

It seems likely, though, that The UMC will decide to maintain its present structures of ordained ministry, including the separate orders of deacons and elders and the commissioning (rather than the ordination) of provisional deacons and elders, and that it will continue to employ increasing numbers of local pastors who are not ordained but who are given sacramental authority in the churches or charges to which they are appointed. It will then become even more important to heed the call to "be clear about the forms of ministry we have created and openly acknowledge our uniquely United Methodist

---

24 Anderson, "Postscript: Elders and Local Pastors," 3–4.
25 Campbell, "The Oral Roberts Option."

ordering of ministry, even if it means straining our ecumenical dialogue."[26]

In the wake of the failure, or refusal, of the 2012 and 2016 General Conferences to enact any significant legislative changes related to ministerial orders and sacramental authority based on the recommendations of the previous Ministry Study Commissions, the 2016 General Conference authorized and the Council of Bishops has constituted a new Study of Ministry Commission for the 2016–2020 quadrennium. Perhaps the biggest challenge facing this commission is the pressing need to develop a consistent and coherent theology of ordination, ministerial orders, and sacramental authority to undergird the ministry and mission of The UMC—and then to secure approval by the 2020 General Conference of the legislation necessary to implement that theology in the life and practice of the Church.

This sort of work has been going on in The United Methodist Church since its formation in 1968 and, before that, well back into the history of The Methodist Church. With rare exceptions, there has been a committee or commission appointed to study ministry in the Church in every quadrennium since 1944. Dick Heitzenrater prepared a study in 1988 for the General Board of Higher Education and Ministry, providing "A Critical Assessment of the Ministry Studies since 1944." In one particularly relevant paragraph, Heitzenrater said this concerning the ministry studies conducted between 1944 and 1988:

> There has been a great deal of waffling back and forth on the matter of the nature and purpose of ordination. The matter of orders as distinguished from offices has

---

26 Harnish, *The Orders of Ministry in The United Methodist Church*, 90.

never been made clear in any official statement. The clarity in the earlier reports in distinguishing between clergy and laity on the basis of ordination has now been significantly clouded by the emphasis on general ministry into which one is "ordained" by baptism. And the connection between ordination and the sacraments, already a problem at the outset of these studies, has been alternately clarified, confused, clarified, disregarded, and has generally fallen victim to practical and political pressures quadrennium by quadrennium. A return to the traditional requirement of ordination for anyone who would administer the sacrament was not only short-lived, but was reversed to the extent that lay administration (under certain minimal restrictions) has become commonplace. Whether ordination is essentially a gift of God or a rite of the Church has been voted back and forth by more than one General Conference. Ordination as the mark of a clear distinction between laity and clergy was certain for the first two decades of this period, but that clarity disappeared into the fogginess of representative ministry.[27]

Plus ça change, plus c'est la même chose. It is simply stunning to realize that Heitzenrater wrote that paragraph in 1988, almost three decades ago now. The 1996 ministry legislation that established the permanent order of deacons and introduced the practice (and rite) of commissioning of provisional

---

27 Richard P. Heitzenrater, "A Critical Assessment of the Ministry Studies since 1944," GBHEM Occasional Papers no. 76 (September 1, 1988): 11; http://www.gbhem.org/sites/default/files/documents/publications /occ_076Heit zenrater_0.pdf; also in Russell E. Richey, et al., eds., *Perspectives on American Methodism* (Nashville: Kingswood Books, 1993), 431–47.

elders and deacons has only served to deepen the collective "fogginess" of The UMC about the nature and meaning of ordination and its relationship to ministerial orders and sacramental authority. The increasing reliance of The UMC on the service of unordained local pastors has done nothing to diminish that "fogginess." And in this context, another paragraph from Heitzenrater's 1988 article seems surprisingly apropos today:

> It is easy . . . to blame the process by which our church proceeds in its attempts at official self-understanding and operation. Nearly everything is up for grabs every four years at General Conference. And given the increasingly large and diverse nature of our church, the possibility of focused concerns and real unity seems to fade farther into the background behind the activities of pressure groups and specific interest groups. The political realities of our situation are often mirrored in the membership of significant committees, and the outcome of some committee deliberations naturally tend to reflect the makeup of the committee.[28]

An article by Para Drake on the work of the 2013–2016 Commission for the Study of Ministry characterized it as seeking "open, honest dialogue; a deeper assessment of ministry; and plans for further theological inquiry with other commissions of The United Methodist Church." Further, according to the article, "the ordering of lay ministry, the confusion around the ministry of the ordained deacon, and the challenges inherent in two systems of pastoral education and formation emerged

---

28 Heitzenrater, "A Critical Assessment of the Ministry Studies Since 1944," 12.

as themes for theological reflection."[29] Those challenges still face the 2017–2020 Commission for the Study of Ministry. Everyone associated with The UMC should offer up devout prayers for the members of this commission and the success of their work as they seek to deal creatively and responsibly with the tangled threads of our long and complicated history of struggle with issues related to ordination, ministerial orders, and sacramental authority.

---

29 Para Drake, "Study of Ministry Commission: Theologically Underpinning Leadership" (November 15, 2013); https://www.gbhem.org/article/study-ministry-commission-theologically-underpinning-leadership.

Selected
Bibliography

Bangs, Nathan. *From the Year 1793 to the Year 1816* Vol. 2, *A History of the Methodist Episcopal Church*. New York: T. Mason & G. Lane, 1839.

Behney, J. Bruce, and Paul L. Eller. *The History of the Evangelical United Brethren Church*. Edited by Kenneth W. Kruger. Nashville: Abingdon Press, 1979.

Bucke, Emory S., gen. ed. *The History of American Methodism*. 3 vols. New York & Nashville: Abingdon Press, 1964.

Campbell, Dennis M. "Ministry and Itinerancy in Methodism." In *The Oxford Handbook of Methodist Studies*, edited by William J. Abraham and James E. Kirby, 262–69. New York: Oxford University Press, 2009.

Campbell, Dennis M. *Who Will Go for Us? An Invitation to Ordained Ministry*. Nashville: Abingdon Press, 1994.

Campbell, Ted A. "The Oral Roberts Option: The Case for Ordained Local Elders (and Local Deacons?) in The United Methodist Church." *Quarterly Review* 24, no. 4 (Winter 2004): 358–66.

Coke, Thomas, and Francis Asbury. *The Doctrines and Discipline of the Methodist Episcopal Church in America, with Explanatory Notes*. 10th ed. Philadelphia: Printed by Henry Tuckness, 1798. Referenced in text as MEC *Discipline* 1796.

Drinkhouse, Edward J. *History of Methodist Reform Synoptical of General Methodism 1703 to 1898, With Special and Comprehensive Reference to its Most Salient Exhibition in the History of the Methodist Protestant Church.* 2 vols. Baltimore: Board of Publication of the Methodist Protestant Church, 1899.

Drury, A. W. *History of the Church of the United Brethren in Christ.* Dayton: Otterbein Press, 1924.

Durbin, Linda M. "The Nature of Ordination in Wesley's View of the Ministry." *Methodist History* 9 (April 1971): 3–20.

Emory, Robert. *History of the Discipline of The Methodist Episcopal Church.* 5th ed., revised and updated to 1856 by W. P. Stickland. New York: Carleton & Porter, 1857.

Frank, Thomas Edward. *Polity, Practice, and the Mission of The United Methodist Church.* 2006 ed. Nashville: Abingdon Press, 2006.

Harnish, John E. *The Orders of Ministry in The United Methodist Church.* Nashville: Abingdon Press, 2000.

Heitzenrater, Richard P. "A Critical Assessment of the Ministry Studies since 1944." GBHEM Occasional Papers no. 76 (September 1, 1988): 431–47. Also in Russell E. Richey, et al., eds., *Perspectives on American Methodism.* Nashville: Kingswood Books, 1993.

Heitzenrater, Richard P. *Wesley and the People Called Methodists.* 2nd ed. Nashville: Abingdon Press, 2013.

Holifield, E. Brooks. "Clergy." In *The Cambridge Companion to American Methodism*, edited by Jason E. Vickers, 171–87. New York: Cambridge University Press, 2013.

Holifield, E. Brooks. *God's Ambassadors: A History of the Christian Clergy in America.* Grand Rapids: Wm. B. Eerdmans, 2007.

Lawrence, William B. *Ordained Ministry in The United Methodist Church*. Nashville: Abingdon Press, 2011.

Maddox, Randy L. "Ordained Ministry in The United Methodist Church: Some Historical/Theological Perspectives on Present Concerns." Unpublished presentation to the 2013–2016 UMC Ministry Study Commission at its meeting in Durham, NC, 28–30 October 2013. Used with permission.

Peterson, P. A. *History of the Revisions of the Discipline of the Methodist Episcopal Church, South*. Nashville: Publishing House of the M. E. Church, South, 1889.

Richey, Russell E. *Extension Ministers: Mr. Wesley's True Heirs*. Nashville: General Board of Higher Education and Ministry, UMC, 2008.

Richey, Russell E., Kenneth E. Rowe, and Jean Miller Schmidt, *A History* Vol. 1, *The Methodist Experience in America*. Nashville: Abingdon Press, 2010.

Sherman, David. *History of the Revisions of the Discipline of the Methodist Episcopal Church*. New York, Nelson & Phillips, 1874.

Stuhlman, Byron. *Occasions of Grace: An Historical and Theological Study of the Pastoral Offices and Episcopal Services in the BCP*. New York: Church Publishing, 1995.

Tigert, Jno. J. *A Constitutional History of American Episcopal Methodism*. 4th ed., revised and enlarged. Nashville & Dallas: Publishing House of the Methodist Episcopal Church, South, Smith & Lamar, Agents, 1911.

Warner, Laceye C. *The Method of Our Mission: United Methodist Polity and Organization*. Nashville: Abingdon Press, 2014.

Westerfield Tucker, Karen B. *American Methodist Worship*. New York: Oxford University Press, 2001.

CPSIA information can be obtained
at www.ICGtesting.com
Printed in the USA
FFOW02n2049100418
46233967-47593FF